Landscapes of
Eastern
CRETE

a countryside guide
Third edition

Jonnie Godfrey
and
Elizabeth Karslake

SUNFLOWER BOOKS

Third edition 1999
Sunflower Books™
12 Kendrick Mews
London SW7 3HG, UK

ISBN 1-85691-111-X

Colours of Crete

Important note to the reader

We have tried to ensure that the descriptions and maps in this book are error-free at press date. The book will be updated, where necessary, whenever future printings permit. It will be very helpful for us to receive your comments (sent in care of the publishers, please) for the updating of future printings.

We also rely on those who use this book — especially walkers — to take along a good supply of common sense when they explore. Conditions change fairly rapidly on Crete, and **storm damage or bull-dozing may make a route unsafe at any time**. If the route is not as we outline it here, and your way ahead is not secure, return to the point of departure. **Never attempt to complete a tour or walk under hazardous conditions!** Please read carefully the Country code on page 11 and the notes on pages 47-54, as well as the introductory comments at the beginning of each tour and walk (regarding road conditions, equipment, grade, distances and time, etc). Explore **safely**, while at the same time respecting the beauty of the countryside.

Cover: Panagia Kera, near Kritsa
Title page: Spinalonga Island, from Plaka

Photographs by Elizabeth Karslake, with the exception of page 67 (John Seccombe) and 61, 102 (Deborah Edwards)
Line drawings of island flora by Sharon Rochford
Maps by John Underwood, based on the two-sheet 1:100,000 map of Crete published 1997 by Harms Verlag (with permission)
A CIP catalogue record for this book is available from the British Library.
Printed and bound in the UK by Brightsea Press, Exeter

10 9 8 7 6 5 4 3 2 1

❋ Contents ⸻

☀ Preface

Mere mention of Crete conjures up all sorts of shimmering images, and we hope that our book — covering the eastern end of the island — will give you the key to some of Crete's mystery and majesty.

The landscapes will hold you spellbound. The surrounding sea — all its vivid shades of blue sparkling in the sun — is part of the scenery too; impossible to separate from the landscape, it's always just in sight, or round the next corner, or disappearing into the skyline.

Woven into the countryside, the people of Crete are yet another part of the landscape. Just a short distance away from all the hubbub and commercialism that a coastline so often creates, a timeless way of life still goes on. Pastoral labours, such as threshing and winnowing, are still carried on without the help of machines. Water is still drawn up from wells.

Whether you walk, drive or picnic in Eastern Crete, the mountains will be your constant companions, changing colour and mood from dawn to dusk, as you move through them, round them and over them. You cannot fail to feel their dramatic attraction.

The stunning colours and heady scent of flowers and herbs, tucked into rough ground or splashed across a hillside, the warm-sounding buzz of hovering bees, and the massed band of a thousand cicadas will all leave a lasting impression — the 'special effects' of the total scene.

You may share this rural bliss only with a solitary shepherd, his flocks and dogs, as you walk the hillsides of Eastern Crete. Greeks, on the whole, don't walk, unless they have to for their day's labour, so be prepared for incredulous looks from the townspeople and faint smiles from the villagers — although over the years they have become accustomed to seeing people passing through clasping the *Landscapes* guide and, knowingly, will point the way from their *cafeneion* seats or smallholdings!

As there aren't any large-scale maps available, we've had some fun just *finding* the walks, let alone convincing Cretans that we really *wanted* to walk and that other like-minded people were going to come and glory in their countryside as a result of our endeavours.

For Elizabeth and me, compiling the various editions of this book together over the years has been a fitting combination and one that will, we are sure, be of benefit to you. Originally it was Elizabeth's first acquaintanceship with Crete and she was able to look at it with an inquiring freshness. I, on the other hand, had left a bit of my soul and a lot of my heart there, having lived and worked on the island in the past, so my experience and knowledge was rife with bias! Within days, Elizabeth was immersed in and enchanted by the 'landscape' — and by that I mean the complete 'feeling' of Crete — as well. We're sure you'll share our delight exploring the east and will follow us from here to the *Landscapes of Western Crete*, if you haven't already joined us there.

— JONNIE GODFREY

Acknowledgements
We would like to express our thanks to the following people for their invaluable help:

Andonis Panayotopoulos, Managing Director of the Istron Bay Hotel, who never questioned the possibility and fostered every step.

Charlotte Davis, who went to great lengths to help us in the early stages and whose 'walk-finding' ability was indispensable.

Kostas Kokkinis, for whose bemused encouragement and unquestioning help we are most grateful.

Hilary and Phil Dawson, Steve Godfrey, Pamela Karslake, Philippa Varney, Marie Karslake, Natalia Karapanagioti and Dimitris Xenakis, Deborah Edwards, Rothes Currie, Chris Field, Maria Kafedzaki and the Istron Bay Hotel staff for invaluable input and support.

Zodiak/Budget Car Rental for frequent four-wheeled support.

Caroline Crittall for introducing us to one another.

Pat Underwood, our publisher, for her enthusiasm and patience with Greek idiosyncracies.

Books you may find useful
Adam Hopkins: *Crete: Past, Present & Peoples*
John Bowman: *The Travellers' Guide: Crete*
Pat Cameron: *The Blue Guide: Crete*
Nikos Kazantzakis: *Zorba the Greek*
Oleg Polunin: *The Concise Flowers of Europe*
John Fisher: *The Rough Guide to Crete*

*Elizabeth (left) and Jonnie ,
in the gorge at Kato Zakros*

❋ Getting about ____

Hiring a car is certainly the best way to get to know the richness of Eastern Crete. We hope that by giving you some good itineraries, you will be able to make the most of the island — and your car. Many of the tours we suggest take you past the starting- and/or end-points of walks. In fact, seeing the countryside from a car will encourage you, we hope, to go off the beaten track and into the hills with us, on foot.

Taxis are an alternative way to tour and, if shared, can be a reasonably-priced way to travel. Do agree a fare before you set out, if it's going to be an unmetered journey. Your holiday company's agent or representative will help you to find a driver who speaks English and who will be happy and proud to show off his island.

Organised excursions are good value on Crete and the coaches eat up kilometres easily while you sit back and watch it all go by.

One of the most entertaining ways of getting about is by **local bus**. Once you've done it for the first time, you'll realise it's economical, reliable and fun! You'll whizz along the highways and bumble through villages with a bus-eye view over the countryside. The plans on pages 8-9 show you where the bus stations are in Agios Nikolaos and Iraklion. Timetables are on pages 133-134 and cover the eastern half of the island. *Please be sure to pick up a current bus timetable at the station before you plan a trip; changes are frequent.* For complete assurance, verify the times by asking. Arrive well before departure time, too, as buses leave promptly or even earlier than scheduled! Buses aren't numbered, but the destination is shown on the front. It's better to buy your ticket in the depot before travelling. The ticket will have a seat number on it, but don't be too adamant about this, as the local people do not, as a rule, adhere to the system themselves. If you buy tickets on the bus, don't be confused if you get as many as three per person for just one trip — they add up to the total. In principle, you can flag down buses en route, but they don't *always* stop. *Do* always put your hand out, even at a bus stop!

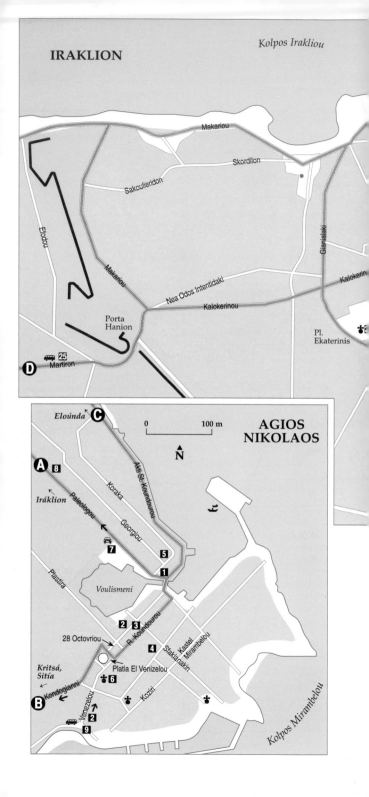

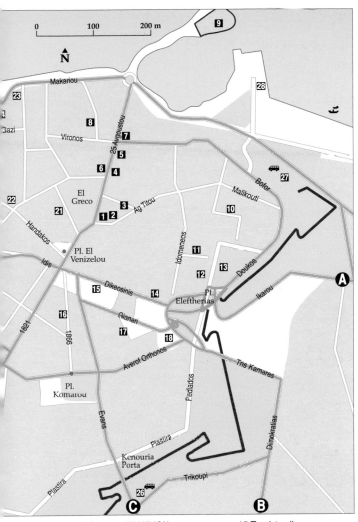

AGIOS NIKOLAOS

1 Tourist information
2 Post office
3 Olympic Airways
4 OTE (telephones, telegrams)
5 Youth hostel
6 Agía Triáda Church
7 Car park
8 Archaeological museum
9 Bus station
10 Car park

IRAKLION

1 Venetian Loggia
2 City hall
3 Agios Títos
4 Swedish consulate
5 Dutch consulate
6 Danish consulate
7 Finnish consulate
8 Norwegian consulate
9 Venetian fort
10 French consulate
11 Consulates of the UK and Germany
12 Tourist information
13 Archaeological museum
14 Alpine Club

15 Tourist police
16 Street market
17 Post office
18 Olympic Airways
19 Agía Ekaterína (museum)
20 Agios Mínas Cathedral
21 OTE (telephones, telegrams)
22 Youth hostel
23 Agios Pétros
24 Historical museum
25 Haniá Gate buses
26 Oasis buses
27 Main bus station
28 Port authority

❀ Picnicking

Picnicking on Crete is not an organised affair. There aren't any specially-provided sites; it's very much a case of pick your own olive tree and toss for the best views! But following is a selection of some good places to throw down a towel or a rug (it's unlikely to be wet, but it might well be prickly) and revel in the countryside.

There are 14 picnic suggestions. All have been chosen for ease of access and none involves too much climbing or lugging of provisions! Picnics 1-10 are along the routes of walks, and the exact location of each is shown on the relevant *walking* map by the symbol *P;* the nearest bus stop (🚌) and parking place (🚗) are also indicated. You can get to these picnics by car or bus (although bus scheduling may not always be suitable for picnickers). Picnics 11-14 are not on walking routes; you will find their location on the pull-out touring map. Of these, only Picnic 11 (Gournia) is easily reached by bus. Picnics 7, 9, 10 and 12-14 are best saved for days when you're touring by car.

To help you choose a picnic place that appeals to you, some of the picnic settings are illustrated.

If you are travelling to your picnic by bus, be sure to arm yourself with the latest bus timetables. There are bus timetables on pages 133-134, but do remember that no book can ever be as up-to-date as the timetables you can obtain at bus stations.

If you are travelling to your picnic by car, be extra vigilant off the main roads; children and animals are often in the village streets and may not be accustomed to traffic. Without damaging plants, do park *well off* the road; *never* block a road or track.

All picnickers should read the Country code opposite and go quietly in the countryside.

1 KRITSA OVERLOOK FROM THE NORTHEAST (map pages 56-57, photograph page 34)

🚗 by car: no walking necessary. Follow Car tour 6 or 9 and take the road to Lato, just before Kritsa. Go straight over two crossroads and over a small bridge to the right. After a short slope, the road curves round to the left. Park into the side. Good view of Kritsa.

🚌 by bus: under 30 minutes' walking. Take a bus to Kritsa (Timetable 3) follow Walk 1 as far as the bridge (20min). Then continue up the road towards Lato, to where the road curves to the left.

A country code for walkers and motorists

Observance of certain unwritten rules is essential when out walking or driving in the countryside anywhere, but particularly on Crete's rugged terrain, where irresponsible behaviour can lead to dangerous mistakes. Whether you are an experienced rambler or not, it is important to adhere to a country code, to avoid causing damage, harming animals, or even endangering your own life.

- **Do not take risks.** Do not attempt walks beyond your capacity and do not wander off the paths described if there is any sign of enveloping cloud or if it is late in the day.
- **Do not walk alone** and *always* tell a responsible person *exactly* where you are going and what time you plan to return. On any but a very short walk near villages, be sure to take a compass, whistle, torch, extra water and warm clothing, as well as some high energy food, like chocolate. This may sound 'over the top' to an inexperienced walker, but it could save your life.
- **Do not light fires**; everything gets tinder dry. If you smoke, make absolutely sure your cigarettes are completely extinguished.
- **Do not frighten animals.** The goats and sheep you may encounter are not used to strangers. By making a noise, trying to touch or photograph them, you may cause them to run in fear and be hurt.
- **Walk quietly** through all farms, hamlets and villages, and leave all gates just as you found them, wherever they are. Although animals may not be in evidence, the gates *do* have a purpose.
- **Protect all wild and cultivated plants.** Don't pick fruit if it looks like it is somebody else's livelihood. You'll doubtless be offered some en route, anyhow. Avoid walking over cultivated land.
- **Take all your litter** back with you and dispose of it somewhere suitable.
- When **driving**, never block roads or tracks. Park where you will not inconvenience anyone or cause danger.

Donkey trail near Pines

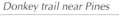

2 KRITSA OVERLOOK FROM THE SOUTHEAST (map pages 56-57)

🚗 by car: about 25 minutes on foot. Follow Car tour 6 to Mardati and park by the buildings on the left, on the only bend in the road. Then follow Walk 3.

🚌 by bus: about 25 minutes on foot. Take a bus to Mardati (Kritsa bus, Timetable 3) and follow the start of Walk 3.

3 HILLS ABOVE VASILIKI (map pages 76-77; photographs page 78)

🚗 by car: under 20 minutes on foot. Follow Car tour 1 as far as Pahia Ammos. At 22km turn right for Ierapetra. At 24km, opposite a gorge at Monastiraki, turn right to Vasiliki. Park in the main street; then follow Walk 7.

🚌 by bus: under 40 minutes on foot. Take the Ierapetra bus (Timetable 5) as far as the Vasiliki turn-off; then follow Walk 7.

4 HIGH OVER SPINALONGA AND KOLOKITHIA
(map pages 70-71; photograph pages 68-69)

🚗 by car: under 5 minutes on foot. Follow the notes for Car tour 5 from Plaka. Some 5km outside Plaka, en route to Vrouhas, take a right-hand turning just before a church and some eye-catching corn mills. Park here and then follow the track to the right for a few minutes.

🚌 by bus: about 30 minutes on foot. Take a bus to Plaka (Timetable 7) and follow Walk 5.

5 OVERLOOKING ELOUNDA (map pages 70-71)

🚗 by car: just 3-4 minutes on foot. Follow Car tour 5 to Elounda, then take the road out of the village towards Pano Elounda (leaving the clock tower on your right). Look out for a concrete track down to the right and a small donkey trail up to the left (a small white church is just visible up the trail). Parking safely is difficult; get as far off the road as you can. Then it's just a few minutes' walk up the trail.

🚌 by bus: 25-30 minutes on foot. Take a bus to Elounda (Timetable 2) and follow Walk 6.

6 BESIDE THE SEA AT MAKRIGIALOS (map page 100)

🚗 by car: no walking. Follow Car tour 1 for 99km, to the pleasant sandy beach at Makrigialos, where Walk 13 begins and ends. Swim or dabble your toes on this one.

🚌 by bus: no walking. Ierapetra/Sitia bus to Makrigialos (Timetable 10).

7 NEAR KALAMAFKA (map page 66)

🚗 by car only: 5 minutes on foot (bus timings are unsuitable for picnickers). Follow Car tour 3 to Kalamafka. Leave your car near the bridge and use the notes for Walk 4 from the 10min-point, to follow the rough track to Kefalavrisi, the head of a spring.

8 THE WAY TO THRIPTI (map pages 76-77)

🚗 by car: from 15 to 30 minutes on foot. Follow Car tour 1 to Kavousi. Park in the village, and use the notes for Walk 8 for 15-30 minutes.

🚌 by bus: from 15 to 30 minutes on foot. Take the Sitia bus to Kavousi (Timetable 6) and follow Walk 8 for 15-30 minutes.

9 OVERLOOKING LASITHI FROM THE EAST (map pages 106-107)

🚗 by car only: about 10 minutes on foot (bus timings are unsuitable for picnickers). Follow Car tour 7 for 43km. Then take the track off left, on a bend. Park and walk along the track/donkey trail for about 10 minutes, until you find an appealing spot.

This picture was taken near Kalo Horio on Walk 3, but the setting is typical of many pleasant picnic places on the island.

10 OVERLOOKING LASITHI FROM THE NORTH
(map pages 116-117; photograph page 27)

🚐 by car only: up to 30 minutes on foot (bus timings are unsuitable for picnickers). Follow Car tour 7. Having almost completed the circuit of the plateau, at 64km go straight on for Tzermiado. When you see the sign for this village, take the concrete track to the left, just past the sign. (The track is signposted to Timios Stavros Church). Either park straight away or, if you don't mind driving on a rough track, continue uphill. Picnic at the beginning of the higher plain. Depending on how far you drive, allow up to 30 minutes on foot.

11 GOURNIA (Dorian site, shown on the touring map)

🚐 by car: about 15-20 minutes on foot. Park at Gournia (Car tour 1). Walk back along the main road from the site heading towards Agios Nikolaos. After a few minutes, take the track up left, walking towards the church. Follow this track for 15 minutes or so.
🚌 by bus: about 15-20 minutes on foot. Take the Ierapetra or Sitia bus to Gournia (Timetables 5 and 6). Then follow the notes above for those who come by car.

12 KATHARON PLATEAU (east of Lasithi, shown on the touring map)

🚐 by car only: about 5-10 minutes on foot. Follow Car tour 6 to Avde- liako and park by the *cafeneions*. Walk left (as you look at the *cafeneion* furthest away). Pass the spring water tapped into the wall on the right and continue for 5-10 minutes, to a view of the converging riverbeds and the pastureland beyond.

13 VATHYPETRO (Minoan site, shown on the touring map)

🚐 by car only: no walking. Follow Car tour 10 to Vathypetro and picnic at the site itself, enjoying wonderful views.

14 CRETAN COUNTRYSIDE (see Car tour 9 on the touring map)

🚐 by car only: no walking. Follow Car tour 9 for 20km. Park well into the side. *Note: This tour is recommended for confident drivers only.*

● *Touring*

Crete is a very large island, and most visitors hire a car for some part of their stay to get to grips with it.

It pays to hire for a minimum of three days and, although you may find cheaper rates with small companies, do think what you're paying for with the better-known firms. The larger companies offer the advantage of representation all over the island. Since it's likely that you'll want to cover a lot of ground, you'll be in a better position hiring from a well-known company should anything go wrong en route.

Remember that tyres are *not* covered by insurance; you won't be charged for a simple puncture, but ruined tyres will have to be paid for! Check the car before you set off, and make sure you've got a spare and a jack (often under the bonnet). Be sure you understand the terms of the hire contract you have signed (of course this should be available in English). Keep your hire contract and driving licence with you at all times when out on the road. It's worth taking note of the car hire company's telephone numbers as well, just in case.

Our car touring notes are brief; they include little information readily available in standard guidebooks or the handouts you can obtain free from tourist offices and tourist information kiosks at home or on Crete. Instead, we've concentrated on the 'logistics' of touring: times and distances, road conditions, and giving clear directions where you might falter or be misled using other existing guides. Most of all, we emphasise possibilities for **walking** and **picnicking**. While some of the suggestions for short walks and picnics may not be suitable during a long car tour, you may find a landscape that you would like to explore at leisure another day.

The pull-out touring map is designed to be held out opposite the touring notes and contains all the information you will need outside the towns. The tours have been written up with Agios Nikolaos as departure/return point, but they could quite easily be joined from other centres. Plans of Agios Nikolaos and Iraklion, with city exits, are on pages 8-9.

Some points worth noting

We cannot stress too strongly the advantage of taking with you a good guide to Crete's history and archaeological heritage; see page 6. Note also:

— **Allow plenty of time for visits**; the times we give for the tours include only very brief stops at viewpoints labelled (☞) in the notes.

— **Telephones**, with meters, are located at most kiosks, at OTE (telephone exchanges) and in *cafeneions.*

— WC indicates **public toilets**; these are rare, but others are found in restaurants.

— Don't be flummoxed by **Greek road signs**; they are almost invariably followed by English ones.

— You are meant to cross a **solid white line near the edge of the road**, when someone wants to overtake. However, beware of slower vehicles, laden donkeys, bikes, etc ahead, when you round corners.

— Conversely, **a solid white line in the middle of the road** means NO OVERTAKING — regardless of the behaviour of motorists who appear not to notice it.

— **Do think** before you pull up to admire a view, if you are not at a viewpoint with parking; remember that other motorists cannot see round corners.

— Never throw **cigarette ends** out of the car.

— Come to a standstill at **stop signs**.

— The spelling of **village names** may vary. We have used the letter 'H' where an 'X' or 'CH' might be used locally; this is to aid pronunciation.

— In towns, only **park** your car where permitted.

— **Priority signs** (red/black/white arrows) on narrow stretches of road give priority to the black arrow.

— You will see **shrines** in various places (little boxes often carrying a cross and filled with oil, a candle, an icon, pictures, etc). They warn travellers that sometime in the past a fatal or near-fatal accident involving motor vehicles has occurred at that spot. **Drive carefully!**

Distances quoted are *cumulative km* from Agios Nikolaos. A key to the symbols in the notes is on the touring map. Do note, however, that only the largest churches — or churches that are landmarks — have been highlighted, since every village has at least one church. The same can be said of tavernas or *cafeneions;* food and drink can be found almost anywhere.

All motorists should read the Country code on page 11 and go quietly in the countryside. *Kalo taxithee!*

1 THE NORTH AND SOUTH COASTS

Agios Nikolaos • Gournia • Pahia Ammos • Sitia • Piskokefalo • Lithines • Ierapetra • Episkopi • Agios Nikolaos

162km/100mi; 4 hours' driving; Exit B (or Exit A) from Agios Nikolaos

On route: Picnics (see pages 10-13): (2, 3), 6, 8, 11; Walks (3, 7), 8, (9), 10, 11, 13

This 'grand tour' will highlight for you the contrasting landscapes of the north and south coasts. The roads are in good condition. Although the drive from start to finish takes over four hours, it's an excellent day's outing, with good opportunities for swimming and relaxing in varied scenery, or for short walks to fine viewpoints.

To leave Agios Nikolaos by Exit B, take the road that leads from the village 'square' (the roundabout at the top of the main street). After going over a small bridge when you leave the one-way system (🚲), turn left on the Sitia road. Alternatively you could leave by Exit A: cross the bridge on the harbour and go up the hill to the crossroads at the traffic lights and turn left onto the Sitia road there.

Either way, you pass by the turn-off to Kritsa and Mardati. From Mardati a 25-minute walk would take you to wonderful views over Kritsa and the Lasithi mountains (Picnic 2). Go on via Almiros and Amoudara, the two beaches (often crowded in high season) just outside Agios Nikolaos that keep the occupants of the many surrounding villas and apartments happy, with their cool, spring-filled bays.

Head on through an area known as Agios Silas and then at 11km pass the turning to the old village of Kalo Horio (🚲), where Walk 3 ends. (Car tour 3 turns off here.) This area would be a good place to stop on your return to Agios Nikolaos, for a good Greek meal at Zygos or an excellent fish dinner at Kavos Taverna, just beyond, in Istron. A kilometre further on you'll go by the luxurious Istron Bay Hotel (🏨✕) — which you won't notice till you've passed it, so attrac-

On the coastal road to Sitia: a myriad of oleander bushes grace the foothills of the Orno range, near Sfaka. Walk 11 takes you up into these hills — which are not as barren as they appear to be (see also photographs on pages 94 and 95).

16

vely has it been concealed. In under 30 minutes pass the sign for Gournia Moon Camping (16km), just beyond which is the Minoan site of **Gournia**★ (19km ⛩wc), where the remains of an entire village straddle the hillside to the right. Here a 15- to 20-minute walk would take you to the setting for Picnic 11.

Not far beyond Gournia, drive through the rather drab village of **Pahia Ammos** (21km ⛽M), where there are some surprisingly good fish tavernas by the sea. It is all set against a superb backdrop — the awe-inspiring Thripti Mountains. Pass the main turning for Ierapetra off to the right (22km) and go straight on towards Sitia (⛽ at 23km). This is a particularly attractive coastal route; the road hugs the hillsides to the right and is never far above the sea to the left. Flowers line the roadside, and the colours and patterns on the hillsides change constantly, as sheer rock and vegetation vie for dominance. Numerous villages are passed, perched on hillsides overlooking the sea (⛽ at 27km).

Kavousi (28km ⚲) is the next pretty village of note, nestling in the hills ahead. Walk 8 starts here and takes you up over those glorious hills, to Thripti. Some 20-30 minutes into this walk, from the setting for Picnic 8, you would enjoy splendid views down over Kavousi. Not far beyond Kavousi, at **Platanos** (30km), the Panorama Taverna is worth a refreshment stop, as the views over the island of Psira are particularly fine.

*The track to Thripti. Although we'
driven it in an ordinary car, we
would recommend 4-wheel drive.*

The road bypasses Lastros
(34km) and then a turn-off left
down to Mohlos on the coast.
Should you wish to detour
down to Mohlos (where you
would see the white scar of
gypsum quarries), it is best to
use the road from the next
village en route, **Sfaka**. Walk
11 begins here in Sfaka and
ends at the village shown on
page 91, **Tourloti**. The two
villages seem no distance apart at all by road, but the walk
makes a pleasant loop through lovely countryside and
farmlands. High above Sfaka, surrounded by wheat fields,
you would look out to the Orno range (see photographs
pages 16-17, 94 and 95).

At 44km bypass Mirsini (☗), where there is a church
with attractive Venetian doorways. Note the fine setting
of the church, too: both the parishioners and the priest
can enjoy some wonderful views! From here we descend
into **Mesa Mouliana** (53km ☗), and then the coastal strip
widens out and the mountains dwindle to mere hills
around **Exo Mouliana** (56km). When you see a hill with
ruined stone windmills on it, you'll know you're ap-
proaching the Sitia Plain. The road leads down again,
gently, through **Hamezi** (57km **M**), where you'll find a
museum containing local antiquities, and past Skopi
(63km ☗), below the road, down to the right.

As you near Sitia the landscape is greener and more
fertile; olive trees and vines abound. Sitia is known for its
sultanas, by the way. After about an hour-and-a-half's
driving, you'll get your first good look at **Sitia★**, a large,
white, sprawling harbour town (68km **⏏☗☗M**WC). It's a
pleasant place to wander round.

From Sitia we take a right turning for Ierapetra (signposted). Beyond **Piskokefalo** (71km ☗), the road winds
through olive groves and low vineyards, and the hills in
between are thickly carpeted with shrubs and bushes. The
road heads gradually uphill, giving good panoramic
views. Before long you pass through **Maronia** (77km), a
village tucked almost out of sight below the road
stretching out before you. Look out for fresh spring water

ᵢing from the fountain by the side of the road.

Go through **Epano Episkopi**; the road rises again, ᵧradually, into rolling hills flanked by pine, eucalyptus and plane trees. At 85km, just before Papagiannides, there is a taverna with a fresh water source. Then the road dips down into the sizeable village of **Lithines**. Six kilometres past here, you'll see the Kapsa Monastery off to the left, before coming to the first seaside village on the south coast, **Pilalimata** (98km). Doubtless you'll drive straight through it, eager to see if the rest of the south coast has anything more inspiring to offer. It has, so press on, past the Sunwing Cresta Hotel (🏔✕) Drop down into **Analipsi** and you'll come to **Makrigialos** (🚐), where Walk 13 begins and ends. What about a swim? There's a pleasant, sandy beach here, with several tavernas strung out along it, inviting you to relax ... or you could picnic in the shade of nearby trees (Picnic 6).

After your break, continue past **Koutsouras** (100km; 🚐 at 101km, 102km). Notice now the first *thermokipos* (literally 'hot gardens') at the edge of what is a large area of market gardening. While all the plastic greenhouses don't enhance the scenery, they have done wonders for the livelihood of the local people. Forced crops of tomatoes, cucumbers, bananas, melons, courgettes, etc have brought considerable wealth to this area in recent years. On the hills to your right fires have devastated the once-magnificent pine forests. The lower slopes have been replanted and the upper slopes retain a barren beauty.

As you leave Koutsouras, the flat road curves along beside the sea, passing pretty **Galini** (111km 🚐) and **Agia Fotia**, where Walk 10 ends. Both villages are quiet, pleasant places to stop for a swim, before continuing on through **Ferma** (114km 🏔✕🚐).

One needs to spend some time in **Ierapetra** (123km 🏧🏔✕🚐⊕Mwc). It's a low-key place, full of good fish tavernas and ice-cream and drinks bars. The town beach is pleasant, with the remains of a grand Venetian castle at one end. Ierapetra is the commercial centre for the plastic greenhouse trade. You'll find a small collection of Minoan *sarcophagi* in the library.

On coming into Ierapetra, you will have noticed a signposted turning right for Agios Nikolaos. Return now to this road (🚐) and head left. The route whisks you across the island at its narrowest point, via a low-lying isthmᵤ (three 🚐). Less than 14 kilometres of good road sepaᵣ the Libyan and Cretan seas from south to north. Sꞟ you be planning to climb Stavromenos (V. 9; photograph pages 84-85), turn right Kato Horio, from where you can drive t Thripti along the track shown on page 18 (but we'd only only recommend it for 4-wheel drive vehicles).

Soon (133km 🐾) come to the bypass for **Episkopi**: it's worth making a foray into this village, to visit the tiny blue-domed Byzantine church shown on page 25. It's a jewel, but easy to miss. You'll find it down to the right of the road, opposite the main village church. Walk 10 begins here, and Walk 7 ends here. The photograph on pages 86-87 was taken not far into Walk 10; like many other photographs in this book, it recalls for us the many pleasures of walking in Eastern Crete.

As you drive through this area, you'll understand why it's such good walking country: just look at those glorious mountains! Pass the turning to Vasiliki (Picnic 3), known for the fine specimens of long-spouted, oddly-coloured ancient pottery found here. Vasiliki is the starting point for Walk 7, which takes you into the foothills of the Dikti Mountains. Again, the photographs on pages 78 sum up the pleasures of being on foot in this superb landscape. Opposite the Vasiliki turn-off, slicing through the Thripti range, is the striking Ha Gorge, above Monastiraki (indicated by a signpost at 137km). Although it's hard to imagine from this vantage point, Walk 8 takes you *behind* the gorge, shown on page 83.

From here you'll soon near the north coast (⛽ at 140km). Turn left and make for **Agios Nikolaos** on your outbound route (162km).

From top to bottom: boatman at Elounda, man at Thripti, woman and young priest at Mesa Potami

2 THE FAR EAST AND KATO ZAKROS

Agios Nikolaos • Sitia • Toplou Monastery • Vai • Palekastro • Kato Zakros • Sitia • Agios Nikolaos

241km/150mi; 6h30min-7h driving; Exit B (or A) from Agios Nikolaos

On route: Picnics (see pages 10-13): (2), 8, 11; Walks (3), 8, 11, 12

This is a marathon, but you will be glad you've done it! As it's a long way, the driving is best shared. Kato Zakros is a nice place to overnight.

This excursion takes you to a monastery, a Minoan site, beaches in contrasting settings and wild countryside — a wonderfully exhilarating, if somewhat tiring, day's outing. Set off as you would for Tour 1 and use the notes starting on page 16 for the first 68 kilometres. On this tour you won't have much time for stops; it will take you well over an hour and a half to reach **Sitia★** (68km ΠΤ⛽ MWC). Stay on the approach road, which curves round left, towards the sea. Either turn left into the town for a drink and a rest, or turn right (⛽), taking the road to Vai, which runs along beside the town beach. The signposting is confusing: you need to take the middle route for Vai (the left is no entry and the right goes to an industrial park!). Following the Vai sign, go down to the coast and then turn right. Continue past Sitia's beach, over a narrow bridge, and past Agia Fotia (71km ⛽), into the low-lying, rugged brown hills and some rather uninteresting countryside, until an extraordinary new 'village' (the Dionysis holiday complex; 78km), springs into view. Thereafter the landscape becomes greener and more interesting with some wonderful large rocks and boulders around. If you're lucky, the heady aroma of wild thyme will be all around you. In early summer it's a deep purple colour and is easily confused with heather.

Now the road twists uphill, following the coastline. At 80km turn left for Toplou. The road climbs up again through barren landscape; you may well have to stop for a herd of goats, hundreds of which belong to the monastery up ahead, **Toplou★** (84km †). The small 17th-century church has a lovely bell tower. Inside are some particularly interesting icons. Beyond its architectural beauty, what impresses one most about Toplou is its splendid isolation. Also interesting is a new windfarm opposite the monastery which can be seen from miles away.

Ten minutes back on the road will bring you in sight of the palm trees at Vai. Go round to the right after the small sign for the village; three kilometres along, come into **Vai★** (94km ✕). If it's the summer season, you may not be able to see the palm tree-fringed sandy beach for people! If you don't mind crowds, this is a good place to have a swim, although sunbeds are expensive and you have to pay to park. But Vai is much prettier out of season, when it's easier to enjoy the tropical-looking beach.

After a quick break, press on. You're bound for one of Crete's gems, and it's important to leave enough time for your visit. Leave Vai's beach and, after a few minutes, turn left. Then take the next left for Palekastro, 10 minutes away. The road passes through cultivated countryside, planted with olive trees and vines.

At **Palekastro** (106km ▲▲✕🍽), on reaching the square, turn back down to the left. Rest assured that this turning leads to Zakros — the signpost appears after a few metres. The road climbs for a while, then continues along a fertile valley. Olive groves abound; imagine how many there must be on the island. This asphalt road weaves its way through interesting small villages set in attractive heathland. First pass through **Lagada,** then **Hohlakies** — which is *really* small — and then climb out of the valley. Come into **Azokeramos**, continue through pretty, open countryside, and then head down again, to **Kelaria,** another tiny hamlet. As you head towards the next village, **Adravasti**, perched on the hillside, the soil changes to a striking wine colour.

At 114km you pass a fresh-water fountain, then suddenly you arrive at **Zakros** (124km ▲▲✕), where Walk 12 begins. There is nothing here of special interest, so carry on through, turning right in the 'square' for Kato Zakros, which really *is* worth the time and distance. As you leave Zakros (🍽), there is a sign indicating a Minoan villa on the right and another sign for Kato Zakros, straight

Evening at Kato Zakros

A priest at Toplou catches up on the news.

on. The surrounding countryside is barren and not overly attractive, so press on to a prettier place! Five kilometres past Zakros (you will have passed the starting point for Alternative walk 12), the road hurtles down the side of a hill, with a ravine on the right and only the sea in sight ahead. Drive carefully for the next four kilometres (watching out for middle-of-the-day visitors), until you come into the delightful composure of **Kato Zakros★** (129km **𝍩**; photograph opposite), with its beautiful bay, beach and peaceful seclusion, only marred by lunchtime coaches. The Minoan site, the Palace of Zakro, is behind the beach. Excavation started here at the beginning of the century, and more work has taken place since 1962, revealing the ruins of a late Minoan palace, all on one level — and easier to 'reconstruct' in the mind's eye than some of the other sites on the island. There are no descriptive plaques, so you will need a standard guide book. Behind the palace, in the gorge shown in the photograph at the bottom of page 98 (Walk 12), there are caves that were used for Minoan burials. Before you explore the site, however, you may well head for the beach, since by this time you're likely to be both tired from driving and famished. Around the bay are several pleasant tavernas with open barbecues for grilled delights; it's particularly pleasant in the evening to sit by the sea and watch supper being cooked. George's Villas, 700m from the beach, offer clean, basic rooms with sea views.

When time runs out, retrace your route up the steep mountainside, back to **Zakros** and on to **Palekastro** (155km). Here turn left into the main square and then keep straight on (**𝍩** left) out towards Sitia, passing the turning for the Toplou Monastery. At **Sitia**, turn left, following signposts for Iraklion and Agios Nikolaos. You'll climb out of Sitia and follow the good asphalt coastal road all the way back to **Agios Nikolaos** — about an hour and a half's driving from here (241km).

3 UP INTO THE HILLS

Agios Nikolaos • Kalo Horio • Kalamafka • Anatoli•
Gra Ligia • Ierapetra • Episkopi • Agios Nikolaos
85km/53mi; 2h30min driving; Exit B (or Exit A) from Agios Nikolaos
On route: Picnic (see pages 10-13): (2, 3); Walks 3, 4, 7, (8, 9), 10
Half of this trip is on winding country roads.

It doesn't take long to reach the south coast from Agios Nikolaos if you just go straight there and back via the main road, abutting the western edge of the Thripti mountain range. But it makes a pleasant change to drive one way through the gentler hills and pretty villages west of this main road.

Leave Agios Nikolaos by using the notes on page 16, heading towards Sitia. Tourism has spread from the hub of Agios (thankfully it hasn't stacked upwards as well), out as far as the main road below Kalo Horio. At 11km (some 15 minutes' driving), turn right at the signposting for Kalo Horio and Kalamafka, and then go left for Prina (also signposted). Almost immediately, you'll notice the change: you're in the Cretan countryside! The road winds up through the old village of **Kalo Horio** (12km ✕). (The lovely shady path from the enchanting village of Kroustas down to the coast below Kalo Horio is shown on page 62; Walk 3.) From here we carry on over pine-covered hills, with a steep drop to one side. Notice the pale colouring of the limestone-based soil.

We pass through **Prina** (16km), perched on a hillside, and keep climbing upwards through olive groves and hills cloaked in clover. **Kalamafka** (25km ✝), where Walk 4 starts, is tucked into a hollow and dominated by its church. One kilometre further on, at a T-junction, turn right, following the sign (hidden on a wall behind you) for Males. Orange and lemon trees flourish in this

Harbour at Agios Nikolaos

Byzantine church at Episkopi

sheltered area; but soon we're climbing through pines and scrub again. Massive rock formations create imposing natural sculptures, and a few minutes' driving past Kalamafka there is a wonderful viewpoint to the left of the road (📷); you can look out over the south coast to the Libyan Sea beyond the huge reservoir south of Agios Georgios.

Soon come into **Anatoli** (33km). This is such a pretty village that you may want to stretch your legs by wandering through the maze of alleyways winding down to the left of the road. On the far side of Anatoli, turn left, following the signposting for Gra Ligia. The road snakes quite steeply down the mountainside. Pines give way to olive trees as the coastal plain comes completely into view, straight down across the spread of Ierapetra. In 10 minutes, the road evens out and you drive through **Kalogeri**, where there is a stone fountain on the right for fresh spring water. Continue past a pretty church (✝) on the right. As you approach the coast, bamboo proliferates.

It's rather a disappointment to come down to this part of the south coast, after the beauty of the hills behind us. Unattractive plastic greenhouses, full of tomatoes, courgettes, cucumbers, bananas and melons announce the industry of the region. When the *meltemi* wind blows here — at the height of summer — swathes of plastic rip and run riot across the surrounding countryside, before flying into the sea. When you come to the main south coast road (46km), turn left into **Gra Ligia** (🚌) and continue on to **Ierapetra** (50km). From here use the notes on page 19 to visit the town and return to **Agios Nikolaos** by the main north-south road (85km).

Agios Nikolaos • Malia • (Iraklion) • Agii Deka Gortys • Festos • Matala • Houdetsi • (Knossos) • Agios Nikolaos

300km/186mi; over 6 hours' driving; Exit A from Agios Nikolaos

On route: Walk 18

Some open-road driving, but a popular route; be prepared for slow-moving traffic just beyond Iraklion. All on main roads — easy driving throughout. An extension to the main ('national') highway from Agios Nikolaos to Iraklion is being built, to bypass Kokkini Hani and Hersonisos (and eventually Malia). The first section is due to open in May 1999: it runs from Stalida (east of Hersonisos) to just west of Kokkini Hani. The Malia bypass is projected for 2002. You may wish to use the bypass roads for this tour.

Setting out on this tour you may feel, as we do, that you're embarking on a pilgrimage of sorts; there's something very intriguing about Crete's Minoan past. The famous sites are a 'must', on everyone's itinerary. Even if you don't wish to spend a great deal of time at any particular site, this excursion is worthwhile: it takes in all the highlights and follows an exceptionally scenic route. While you *could* return to Iraklion by crossing the island on the main north/south road (and perhaps, if you want more time at the sites you will choose to do this), we'd like you to see a bit more of the countryside, so we have mapped out a different route for your homeward journey.

From Agios Nikolaos, take the main road to Iraklion (Exit A; Paleologou Street). You're swiftly on your way. After about 11km, look up to the left: the highest village you see is Vrises (Walk 14), on the route to Lasithi. No doubt you'll visit this area at some point (it's fine walking country) — perhaps going via Neapolis, which is the next large town you pass, again on the left. The region's courthouse is at Neapolis. The mills you pass by now, ranged up the hill both below and above the road, were used to grind corn. A sign of the times: they're now still. Beyond Neapolis, just before Vrahasi (set up on a hill to the right), go through a short tunnel (17.5km). Walk 18 ends by this tunnel. Remember to switch off your headlights.

Soon go through **Selinari** (21.5km ✝✗wc); the church of Agios Georgios is up above the road. It's worth looking skywards here — you might be lucky enough to see an eagle soaring over the mountains. As you pass the church, the view opens out and the sea comes into sight down at Sisi. At 25km pass a turn-off (🅿wc) back to Vrahasi, and then come to the turn-off right for the archaeological site at Malia (visited in Car tour 7). A new highway is being

uilt to bypass Malia and Hersonisos. For this tour keep
the route heading for Malia itself. The road first goes
hrough the spread of **Malia**★ (29km ▲ ✕ ⬛ ⊕) — some
people like it, others keep going. Its famous crowded
beach is down a side street, off to the right. We move on,
through **Stalida** and past the mammoth Sofokles pot
emporium; then through **Hersonisos** (37km ▲ ✕ ⬛WC),
which has a relatively pleasant waterfront strand on the
other side of all the shops.

Forge ahead, through **Kato Gouves** (⬛). At 47.5km the

View over the Lasithi Plateau from Walk 18

old road strikes off right to Iraklion, via the coast. 匚
island is in view by now. Soon you'll pass Iraklion
nearest good beach, Kokkini Hani. We suggest you by‑
pass Iraklion today. Take the next turning on the right,
after the traffic lights (68km; signposted to Mires). Then
turn right again, under a bridge. Now follow the sign
indicating straight on for Festos ('Phaistos' is another
frequent spelling).

You're on a country road now (🍴 at 72km, 76km), so
the going could be slow. You'll be through **Siva** almost
before you have noticed. At **Venerato** (84km 🍴), pass a
turn-off left to the Paliani Monastery, 2km off the route.
A minute past here, **Avgeniki** offers little else but petrol
stations (⛽). Now the road climbs straight up through the
hills to **Agia Varvara** (94km ⛽). Its chapel, set on a rock,
comes into view some time before the village. Legend has
it (wrongly) that the geometric centre of Crete is close by.

Continuing south, you'll suddenly have an inviting
glimpse of the sea and the south coast with the Asterousia
Mountains (97km 📷) and then, as you curve round to the
left, in front of you there is a far-reaching panorama over
the Mesara Plain — 5km wide and 30km east to west.
Start descending now (⛽ at 104km), following the curving road down to Crete's largest expanse of *flat* land. It's
certainly a fertile splash amidst all the brown mountains.

When you reach **Agii Deka★** (109km ⛲✗🍴M), if you
wish to see the graphic icons in the 16th-century church,
turn left in the village. As you come out of the village,
there is a turn-off left to the (modern) chapel containing
the Tombs of the Ten Cretan Martyrs ('Agii Deka' means
'holy ten'). Then, almost at once, the main road takes you
to **Gortys★** (111km 🏛⛲), a Dorian site of great impor-
tance and once the capital of Crete, with a population that
may have reached 300,000. Legend has it that Zeus and
Europa cavorted here (look for the plane tree where it all
happened). The remains of the Basilica of Agios Titos
stand in front of Gortys: according to the Bible, St Titus
was commissioned by St Paul to convert the Cretans.

From Gortys we continue west through **Kapariana**
(117km ✗🍴wc). Now referring to the map of Western
Crete, continue through **Mires** (118km 🛒✗🍴⊕) and
past the monastery of Panagia Kaliviani (123km), now an
orphanage and convalescent home. Within striking distance of Festos, up on the hill, turn left (125.5km). There
are more good views as you climb above the plain (📷).
Then you reach the high point of today's pilgrimage,

Festos★ (127.5km 🚻✕WC). As you walk from the car to the site, breathe deeply and inhale the scent of pines. And then take in the view! The Minoans certainly knew how to choose their settings. It's a glorious viewpoint towards the Dikti and Lasithi mountains to the east, the Ida range to the north and the Asterousia to the south. At the tourist pavilion you'll find all the information you need to help you make the most of your visit. When you leave, don't miss **Agia Triada★** (🚻), the remains of a summer palace in a delightful setting. To get to it, carry on through the car park at Festos and fork right. This turning will take you back down towards the Mesara Plain, to a spot from where you can walk down to the site in three minutes. Just imagine it: some say the sea came right up to this palace.

When you've had your fill of Crete's fascinating past, you might entertain thoughts of a swim. Anyway, you must see the famous caves of Matala. So take the road back to Festos and, at the junction before the car park, turn sharp right for Matala. There's a pretty church on the left, surrounded by the customary cypresses. Turn right at the T-junction (137km ⛽). **Pitsidia** (139km ✕) is the next pretty village, but **Matala** (143km ⌒🚻🏖✕WC) has a fine sweep of sand. The caves here, once inhabited by hippies, are carved in a high ochre cliff (see photograph below). No one knows who first used them, and they vary in size and 'furnishings'.

When the time comes to head back to Agios Nikolaos, drive off in the direction you came and, at the fork (148km) turn left into **Pitsidia**. (About 1km west of Pitsidia is Komos Beach, a very long, sandy and quiet beach with an important archaeological site by the sea.) Follow the

The beach at Matala

road back to **Festos** (156km) and drive through the car park, back down the main road. Here turn right (158km) at the signpost for Iraklion and head back across the Mesara Plain. One kilometre beyond **Agii Deka**, turn right at the signpost for Pirgos and Gangales (173km). The road travels through olive groves and almond trees. Past the narrow streets of **Gangales** (177km) you glimpse pretty Stoli ahead to the right. The vista across the plain is really magnificent: the greens of the foreground spreading and merging into the browns in the distant mountains. Drive through **Stoli** (182km 🍴) and turn right at the crossroads (left goes to Iraklion). Head on to **Asimi** (186km 🍴), a rather down-at-heel, dusty place. Two kilometres past here, stay on the main road, which curves round to the right; then head straight on, following signs for Viannos. At the T-junction 5km further on (194km), turn left for Iraklion.

Ligortinos (198km 🍴) is up to your right. The landscape around here looks like an embroidery sampler, with all its different stitches, green and brown. The route is straightforward now, through **Tefeli** (199km 🛉🍴), across a narrow bridge at 207km and the dot on the landscape called **Partheni** (211km). Soon you reach **Houdetsi** (215km 🍴), **Agios Vasilios** (217km 🛉) and **Kaloni** (219km). Here turn left on the main road for Iraklion. Very soon you'll see the north coast again, over the brow of a hill. First go through **Peza** (221km 🛉🍴) and **Kounavi** (223km 🛉🍴). Turn right at 229km, heading on towards Spilia. Less than 1km ahead, to your left, is Agia Irini with its attractive aqueduct built during the brief occupation of Crete by the Egyptians in the middle of the 19th century. (There's a very good taverna at the foot of the aqueduct, called 'O Hriazoumenos'). Beyond **Spilia** (231km 🍴) keep a look-out for a brief view of Knossos, hidden away in the cypress trees over to your right.

We suggest that you save your visit to Knossos and the museum at Iraklion for another day (Car tour 10). Certainly your visit to the museum will be more meaningful now that you've seen some of the sites that yielded its treasures. Leaving Knossos on your right (233-235km 🍴), drive into the outskirts of Iraklion. A sign indicates a left turn for Agios Nikolaos, about 100m after some traffic lights (237km). The turn-off is immediately opposite the sign. Go left again at the next crossroads (238km) and you're on the main **Agios Nikolaos** road, re-entering the town after 300km.

5 THE AGIOS IOANNIS PENINSULA

**Agios Nikolaos • Elounda • Plaka • Vrouhas • Loumas
• Skinias • Karidi • Pines • Agios Nikolaos**

60km/37mi; 2h15min driving; Exit A (or Exit C) from Agios Nikolaos

On route: Picnics (see pages 10-13): 4, 5; Walks 5, 6

*Late afternoon sun spreads a wonderful light over this glorious scenery,
but this easy drive can be made at any time of day. Roads are mostly in
good condition. No petrol for 40km beyond Elounda.*

Here's one of the prettiest short drives you could hope
for: it takes you onto the Agios Ioannis Peninsula,
pointing out into the Sea of Crete towards the distant isles
of Karpathos and Rhodes.

If you leave Agios Nikolaos via Exit A, you can take the
old road round the back of the village and turn right at
the main crossroads; then turn right again for Elounda (🏪
at 1km). Or you can drive straight along the sea front in
Agios Nikolaos, past the Minos Beach and Mirabello
hotels, and over a bridge. Then turn up and right onto the
signposted Elounda road. At 5.5km out of Agios Nikolaos
there is a splendid viewpoint (📷) by Adrakos Villas,
looking down over the causeway at Olous, towards
Elounda, and — in the distance — the island of Spinalonga. The Agios Ioannis Peninsula (large-scale map
pages 70-71) stretches beyond Plaka as far as the eye can
see. Driving downhill (🏪 at 7.2km), still taking in the
view, pass the Elounda Beach Hotel and, a little further
on, the Astir Palace — flags aflutter.

Come into **Elounda**★ (9.5km 🏔 ✕⊕; Picnic 5), where
'Who Pays the Ferryman?', a popular TV series of the
1970s, was filmed (as was 'The Lotus Eaters' in the '60s).
Three sides of the village square are given over to tavernas, coffee shops and bars, while the fourth is open to
the sea and usually busy with boats. Elounda is the starting
point for Walk 6. Driving through the village, turn right
behind the church and clock tower. The road hems the
sparkling sea all the way along to **Plaka** (13km ⚓✕), the
starting point for Walk 5. This is one of our favourite
swimming spots (photograph page 74), even though after
enjoying the clear silky-soft water, you have to make yourself comfortable on large rounded stones to sunbathe.

Tear yourself away from Plaka: drive along behind the
beach and start climbing up the long steep hill that cuts
across the mountain. The first curve in the road is where
Walk 6 ends — ideally placed for a swim at Plaka. Some
5km out of the village, take a right-hand turning — just
before a church and some eye-catching corn mills (18km;

31

Harbour and clock tower at Elounda

photograph page 67), and you come to a perfect picnic spot (Picnic 4; photograph pages 68-69). If you park here, you can enjoy Short walk 5 (page 67). Then return to the main road and continue up to **Vrouhas** (19km) A stone-built fountain in the village is good for quenching thirst. Go through the village and continue towards Loumas. Pass a sign for Seles, a village set down off to the right, and drive on up through a landscape almost 'cluttered' with stone walls. Only a few scatterings of shrubs and olive trees are to be seen.

After **Kato Loumas** (22km ♥) carry on to **Pano Loumas**, past more corn mills, through olive groves, and always with the sea in sight. In **Skinias** (26km), turn left at the signpost and blink through the two houses of **Valtos**. The views are beautiful. At 28km the road forks; take the left hand fork, signposted to Karidi. (The right fork goes cross country to Neapolis.) The road makes sharp bends, ravens circle above and, beyond the olive-clad hills, the scenery becomes more barren and shrub-covered. Soon you'll pass the Aretios Monastery, just to the side of the road and, after another bend or two, look down on the red roofs and church of **Karidi** (it means 'walnut'; 37km). It's worth stopping at this village. Set into the hills are stone houses, once luxury accommodation for goats and sheep. This area is a miniature, very fertile plain, with huge stone wells, corn mills — and a friendly *cafeneion*. Back on the road, 1km further on drive through **Dories**, where you'll pass the village reservoir on your left. Keep left through Dories; in a few minutes there's another marvellous view — looking east to the mountains round Kavousi and Thripti, settings for Walks 8 and 9.

Now descend through firs and vines and, at a fork, turn left for Elounda. Soon reach a splendid viewpoint (📷) over Pines and Elounda. Come into **Pines** (43km): the road crosses the path of Walk 6. Continue down the hill past **Pano Elounda** and back into **Elounda** itself (47km). Take a break here, wait for the walkers, and then it's back to **Agios Nikolaos** (60km).

6 FROM HILL VILLAGE TO SHEPHERD COMMUNITY

Agios Nikolaos • Kritsa • Katharon Plateau • Agios Nikolaos

50km/31mi; under 2 hours' driving; Exit B from Agios Nikolaos
On route: Picnics (see pages 10-13): 1, 2, 12; Walks 1, 2, 3, 15
The road from Agios Nikolaos to Kritsa is good and wide. From Kritsa to Katharon almost all the way is currently asphalted but, where it is still unmade, the going is rough and dusty. No petrol for 34km beyond Kritsa.

Another short excursion: this one takes you up from the hubbub of Agios Nikolaos into the heart of the shepherd community in no time. You'll drive steadily upwards until you reach the Katharon Plateau, and on your way back you'll feel you've been a visitor to another world.

Leave Agios Nikolaos by Exit B (🚗 at the junction) and go straight over the crossroads on the road signposted for Kritsa (5km 🚗). You'll pass through **Mardati** — no more than a scattering of houses. Walk 3 starts here; 25 minutes into that walk, the setting for Picnic 2 gives you a lovely outlook over Kritsa and the mountains of Lasithi.

Kritsa and the hills beyond come into sight just before **Panagia Kera★** (👤), the gem of a church shown on page 41 and the cover; it cherishes some 13th-century frescoes. If there is a string of tourist coaches parked here now, go on and hope to have a look on the way back, when there is a chance that the crowd will only consist of *you.*

Just before the one-way system takes you into the centre of Kritsa, the Dorian site of Lato (photograph page 55) is indicated to the right. This is the starting point for Walk 1 and Picnic 1 (see photograph page 34). We're sure you'll want to make a stop at **Kritsa★** (8km ✖🚗; Walks 1, 2 and 15), one of our favourite places. It's an attractive hill village, where some of the *cafeneions* have fantastic panoramic views straight out over the Mirabello Gulf. Don't just stay on the main street, however. Wander up or down behind it and have a closer look. People won't mind, if you greet them pleasantly.

Back in the car, take the right-hand fork uphill through Kritsa. Look for the signpost at the next fork: it directs you on to the **Katharon Plateau**. *Almost immediately,* turn hard left, up another signposted road. This road climbs up and into the hillside behind Kritsa. It's a long pull, but you'll be rewarded by splendid views over the Mirabello Gulf and Kalo Horio. Halfway up, you'll pass a jeep track off right to Tapes — and a second one almost at Katharon. The hillsides are covered with gorse bushes and spiny

Overlooking Kritsa from the northeast (Picnic 1)

shrubs which, as you get higher, tend to look like crouching animals — even people.

Take heart when you're halfway up and wondering if it's going to be worth the effort. The scenery becomes less lunar-like, and soon trees appear, counteracting the starkness. At 19km you lose sight of the sea for a while, and tall trees cluster along the track, making a pleasant change of mood. A few kilometres further on, there is evidence of another 'living planet'. Two kilometres before your goal the asphalt disappears and the plateau begins and, to prove it, there are patches of cultivated land, a small vineyard or two, beehives, and two chapels. Shortly after this, come upon **Avdeliako** (25km) and the welcome sight of two *cafeneions* — one either side of an open area, shaded by walnut trees and overlooking the surrounding countryside (Picnic 12). Do taste the glorious fresh spring water coming out of the wall down some steps to the left of the *cafeneion* furthest away, to the right. If you have a 4-wheel drive vehicle, it's also worth bumping along the track in between the two *cafeneions* as far as you can go (about 2km), passing a small church on the right. Then park and continue uphill for about 35 minutes, to enjoy the fantastic view down over the Lasithi Plateau. Shepherds (sometimes together with their families) live up here from the first days of May until the beginning of winter. The pace is slow and rural; the peace and quiet is heavenly. Don't be surprised if someone gets into your car for the journey back. They are more than likely just going to Kritsa and will be most grateful for the lift.

Returning the same way, you'll be back in **Agios Nikolaos** after 50km.

7 THE LASITHI PLATEAU

Agios Nikolaos • Neapolis • Mesa Potami • Psychro • Krasi • Mohos • Malia • Agios Nikolaos

117km/73mi; about 4 hours' driving; Exit A from Agios Nikolaos

On route Picnics (see pages 10-13): 9, (10); Walks 14-17

Although the route is straightforward, it's a tiring one. Lots of hairpin bends demand cautious driving.

Most people want to see Lasithi. This is a good day's excursion, taking in not only the plateau but some lovely mountain scenery, an archaeological site, and a sandy beach as well.

Leave Agios Nikolaos by Exit A, the Iraklion road (🚗 at 1km). Take the turning off right for Neapolis. As you curve round and over the national road, ignore the sign-posted turning for Skinias/Elounda (visited on Car tour 5); turn left at the next T-junction and right at the BP garage and follow the Lasithi Plateau signs into the large square at **Neapolis** (13km 🏔✖🚗M), with its imposing church. Turn left at the top of the square, by the Laograph Museum, and wind up the hillside. The road is good, although a bit ragged at the edges. You drive through the lush and fertile valley of Lakonia and up past the Kremaston Monastery (✝). Walk 14 visits **Vrises** (16km), a pretty hillside village from where the view over Neapolis to the hills beyond is excellent. Another road comes in from Agios Nikolaos at 20km: here turn right for the Lasithi Plateau. You'll drive through **Kato Amigdali** (24km) and, as you come into **Amigdali** 1km further on, look ahead to the towering mountainside, and you will see the scree that Walk 15 takes you across. It's not too difficult a walk, just long!

The lucky passengers can now enjoy stunning views over the countryside to Mirabello Bay and over the surrounding hills and mountains ahead. The less fortunate driver negotiates hair-pin bends! Moutsounis Café/Bar offers respite at **Zenia** (28km). The hillsides around here are dotted with broom and gorse and, at **Exo Potami** (33km), where there is a church and monument dedicated to war victims, you'll find an even greener landscape, with tall cypress trees, almond, walnut, fruit trees and vineyards. ('Potami' means 'river', which would account for the verdant growth.) **Rousakiana** is next, followed by **Mesa Potami** (36km ✖), where excursion coaches and local buses stop en route for the plateau.

And soon you'll have your first glimpse of the edge of the **Lasithi Plateau★**. At 43km you'll pass a track off to the left on a bend (Picnic 9); Walk 15 from Tapes to Kritsa follows this track for part of the way. Go through **Niki-foridon** and into **Mesa Lasithi** (44km), where Walk 15 starts. Past this village, by a large church on your left (46km ♣), turn left for Psychro. Go through **Agios Kon-standinos.** Keep straight on, leaving a turning back to the main road to Agios Nikolaos off to the left. **Agios Georgios** (48km ♣♥M) has a Cretan folklore museum in its midst — well worth a visit.

Now, as the road starts to climb, the plateau comes into full view, showing off just some of its windmills . Pass through **Avrahontes** (♥ open Sundays), **Kaminaki** (✕), and the narrow street of **Magoulas**. Soon you're in **Psychro** (53km ▲▲✕♥ and freshwater fountain). If you would like to visit the Diktaion Cave, take the road curving up left to a parking area and viewpoint (55km ∩⊡). To really appreciate the windmills of Lasithi, leave your car here and walk a while along the route of easy Walk 16 (photograph page 109).

Continue the tour by returning to the main road that hems the plateau and here turn left (signposted to Kato Metohi). The road goes via **Plati** and **Kato Metohi** (59km). Complete the circuit of the plateau and, at 64km, turn left for Iraklion; the signpost is hidden behind a tree on the right and easily missed, so look out for the turn-off just past the Panorama Taverna. (Go straight on towards Tzer-miado here, however, if you're planning to drive up to the setting for Picnic 10, shown on page 27.) The Vidianis Monastery is off to your left. Up on the hill ahead there are some eye-catching old mills standing sentry on the skyline and marking your departure from the plateau (seen from below on Walk 17). The road climbs and soon there is a panorama far below you, straight over to the north coast (⊡).

Go through **Kera** (66km; start of Walk 17) and past the turning for Moni Kera; then turn right off the road and into **Krasi** (✕wc). It's worth making a short detour here to see the mammoth plane tree — reputed to be the largest in Europe — set in the middle of the village. Opposite it there is a pleasant taverna and a freshwater fountain. Driving on through Krasi, carry straight on at a junction, ignoring a road to the right. You are back on the main road, driving down towards the coast. Olive trees abound in this fertile basin, and in their midst is the pretty village of **Mohos** (♥). Leave this village by heading diagonally across the square.

A taverna lunch in the company of the local people is a pleasant way to break a car tour or walk.

A little way out of Mohos you'll have your first glimpse of the sea and a good view (📷) of the coastline and Stalida Beach below. There is a fairly awesome drop on one side of the road (edged with a crash barrier), so do drive carefully. When you reach the main Iraklion/Agios Nikolaos road at **Stalida** (87km), turn right. If you fancy a swim and some relaxation in the sun before heading back to base, sandy Anthoussa Beach is immediately on your left. **Malia**★ is a little further on (92km 🛉🏖✕🍴⊕). You might like to visit the archaeological site just beyond it, off left (signposted at 93km). A kilometre further on there is a turn-off indicating Sisi/Milatos. The cave at Milatos (⋂𝓟), with its nearby ancient site, was the setting in 1823 of a two-week siege in which over 3600 Cretans were massacred by the Turks.

Continue (🍴 at 95km) through **Selinari** (101 🛉✕WC), and then remember to turn your lights off as you leave the tunnel (102km), homeward bound. There's a good chance to fill up before tomorrow's journey (🍴 at 113km, 115km), before you reach the crossroads at the edge of **Agios Nikolaos** (117km).

8 A CENTRAL SWEEP

Agios Nikolaos • Hersonisos • Kasteli • Panagia • 'Embaros • Ano Viannos • Kato Symi • Ierapetra • Agios Nikolaos

166km/103mi; 3h30min driving; Exit A from Agios Nikolaos

On route: Picnics (see pages 10-13) 3, 6; Walks 4, 8, 9, 10, 19, 20

All on main roads — easy driving throughout. An extension to the main ('national') highway from Agios Nikolaos to Iraklion is being built, to bypass Kokkini Hani and Hersonisos (and eventually Malia). The first section is due to open in May 1999: it runs from Stalida (east of Hersonisos) to just west of Kokkini Hani. The Malia bypass is projected for 2002. You may wish to use the bypass roads for this tour.

This excursion makes a great circling sweep that will ensure you see a good deal of Eastern Crete. We don't lead you off the beaten track on this tour, because there's plenty to see and do without straying far off good roads. Also we think it's much nicer — and more appropriate — to *walk* when you want to go right into the countryside, and this car tour will take you past the start or finish of six walks — you could actually combine two of them with the tour, just to whet your appetite!

Leave Agios Nikolaos by Exit A, picking up the national highway and heading west. Six kilometres beyond **Hersonisos** (🏔🍴), turn left for Kasteli; this turn-off comes up almost immediately after the sign for Kasteli and the Water Splash Fun Park. The road is reasonable, with an asphalt surface; the landscape looks comfortable, the hills are low and covered with bushes. Once in **Kasteli** (55km ✝🏛), turn right at the first T-junction, heading for Viannos. In the main square, turn left, then right — again following signing for Viannos. The road climbs. Soon you will need to take a *right* turn downhill along ΟΔΟΣ ΒΙΑΝΝΟΣ — look for the sign high up on your *left* — it's easy to miss. At 64km come to a maze of road signs: follow those for Viannos which, at the first, second, and third crossroads is indicated as straight on. Four kilometres further on, at **Panagia** (68km), you will notice the mountains of the Dikti range unfolding before you. Panagia is situated in a flat fertile basin, surrounded by clover-clad hills. There's a pretty view looking back over it at 70km (📷).

'Embaros (74km), set off the main road, is where Walk 19 starts and, as you've got a car, why not combine a version of the walk with your tour? You could park at 'Embaros and do the Short walk described on page 120. This would give you an opportunity to stretch your legs, by walking to the top of a gorge from where there is a splendid view (see photograph page 122).

Continuing along the main road, pass through **Thoma-diano**, where running water keeps the vegetation lush. Then, at the sign for Martha (78km), keep straight on up the hill, passing above the village. Before long you'll see a number of signposts (83km): go straight on, to descend gradually, first into **Kato Viannos** (85km; 🚌 at 87km) and then into **Ano Viannos** itself (88km ♣️✗🚌). Walk 19 ends at this village, having crossed up and over the mountains from 'Embaros. Leaving Ano Viannos, cross the bridge

Seascape at Kalo Horio, near the end of the tour

and, by 92km, you'll be able to see down to the sou
coast — over the reddish-brown landscape dotted wit
green (☞). Drive past the memorial to the war dead a
Amiras (94km) and then the turning to Arvi Beach.

A kilometre past **Pefkos** (97km ☎; the name means
'pine'), you'll see a turning left to Kato Symi, a kilometre
off the main road. Here's another opportunity to combine
a walk with the drive. From **Kato Symi** — a pretty leafy
village — you could walk (or drive) up to the Minoan
sanctuary of Hermes and Aphrodite (12km there and
back). Water gushes out from hillside springs on the way
up, so take a drinking container with you to replenish your
supply. (If you are tempted to walk on, beyond the site,
the track continues and eventually flattens out after about
two and a half hours, on a 'summit', where there is a cross-
less church, made out of the local purple slate.)

Back on the main road below Kato Symi, pass a church
on a bend (100km). Acres and acres of trees were burnt
to the ground here in the summer of 1984, but replanting
— and nature — have done a great deal to heal the
landscape. One of our favourite walks, Walk 20, starts at
Mournies. This excursion, illustrated on page 127, would
lead you — via three gorges and masses of beautiful pines
— to Males, higher up in the Dikti range. This isn't a walk
to be done from a car tour however; you would end up
twelve kilometres from where you parked! We pass
below Mournies, continuing along above Mirtos off right.
We now near the plastic greenhouses of the Ierapetra
area, and we go through **Nea Anatoli** and **Gra Ligia.**
Come in to **Ierapetra** (129km **i⊤**▲✕☎⊕Mwc).

From here use the notes starting on page 19 to return
to **Agios Nikolaos** (166km). You'll pass through or nearby
the settings for Picnics 3 and 11, as well as the starting-
or end-points of Walks 7-10 (these walks are illustrated
on pages 78-88). When you reach the north coast, turn
left. You'll have a good view over Gournia and then the
sea around Kalo Horio.

5km/28mi; 1h30min driving; Exit B from Agios Nikolaos

On route: Picnics (see pages 10-13): (1), 2, 14; Walks 1-4, 15

Some of the roads and tracks used on this tour are very rough, better for jeeps than low cars. In places the route is only wide enough for one vehicle, with precipitous drops on the driver's side. So, although it is quite safe to undertake, this is not a trip recommended for nervous drivers or passengers.

Pine trees, pretty villages and lovely sea views are all on your 'doorstep' if you're based in Agios Nikolaos — but you *do* have to know where to go. Most of this tour is on 'country roads', unlikely ever to see the asphalt layers. We make a 'sweep' similar to the route of Walk 3 but, where we use rough tracks today, the walk follows footpaths. Perhaps this foray deep into the countryside will tempt you to try some of our walks.

Leave Agios Nikolaos by Exit B and use the notes starting on page 33 as far as **Kritsa★** (8km ♥✕🍴). As you approach Kritsa, you'll pass the road off right to Picnic 1 and Lato (🎋 — photographs on pages 34 and 55; see Car tour 6). Bear right into the one-way system and continue up into the village. Turn right as you meet the square, pass the bust of Rodante on your left and the church of St John the Theologian on the right, and then turn left. 'Kroustas' is written here in Greek, but it's decipherable. As you climb up out of Kritsa there's a good view (🎦) of the hills in the Thripti range. After 11km you are really quite high up, looking straight onto Kritsa (🎦).

Drive into **Kroustas** (13km ♥) and keep going straight on through and out of the village back onto the rough

Panagia Kera, near Kritsa

Kritsa — away from the tourist.

road. Walk 3 from Mardati brings you into Kroustas via the attractive back streets of the village. Pass beside a dry river bed and go over a bridge — here's where Walk 4 from Kalamafka comes in to Kroustas. When the road divides (15km), take the left fork. Ignore a track going off to the right (16.5km). Half a kilometre further on, continue round to the right and take a track off to the left. A minute further on, keep straight ahead and stay on the main, more obvious track. Soon (at 18km), you'll notice a steep unprotected drop — particularly if you're driving! The track, cut into the mountainside, is only wide enough for one car and would be very unnerving for an unskilled driver or faint-hearted passengers. But the scenery is spectacular!

When the track divides again at 19km, take the right fork (ignoring the sign for Agios Ioannis to the left). It takes you through lovely pine trees and woods, with oleander at every corner (Picnic 14 at 20km). At 21km the track curves round sharply onto the next hill. Soon you will be able to see Kalo Horio, its valley and two bays, down to the left. This must be good bee and honey country, judging from the groups of hives that begin to appear as the pines run out and the olive groves begin.

When you come to the outskirts of Prina, turn left immediately — unless you want to go and look at the village — and go steeply downhill. On reaching the main asphalt road (24km), turn left and soon you'll have a marvellous view of Kalo Horio spread out below you. The turquoise-blue water turns to deep sapphire as your gaze is drawn further out to sea.

The attractive cemetery in the foreground before **Pirgos** will catch your eye. Descend past the village, meet the north coast road below **Kalo Horio** (photograph page 39), and turn left for **Agios Nikolaos** (45km).

...os Nikolaos • (Iraklion) • Knossos • Arhanes • ...thypetro • Kasteli • Agios Nikolaos

63km/101mi; under 3h30min driving; Exit A from Agios Nikolaos

On route: Picnic (see pages 10-13): 13; Walk 18

Most of this tour is on fairly decent country roads. A stretch beyond Iraklion is narrow and requires patient driving if you're behind slow-moving traffic. An extension to the main ('national') highway from Agios Nikolaos to Iraklion is being built, to bypass Kokkini Hani and Hersonisos (and eventually Malia). The first section is due to open in May 1999: it runs from Stalida (east of Hersonisos) to just west of Kokkini Hani. The Malia bypass is projected for 2002. You may wish to use the bypass roads for this tour.

Plan on being out for most of the day, if you want to see Knossos, the museum of Iraklion and Vathypetro. This tour description omits Iraklion from the driving distances and times. Follow the notes for Tour 4 (page 26), choosing whether to use the bypass roads. Pass the turn-offs to the airport and industrial area for Iraklion and, at the traffic lights, turn right for Knossos. (There is only a small sign, almost on the lights, indicating Knossos; the main sign is for Iraklion). Go down the hill and turn right again; Knossos is signposted here (🚇 at 64km, 65km). **Knossos★** (66.5km 🕆✕), the most famous site on Crete, was once the capital of the Minoan kingdom, as you may be aware.

After your visit, continue on the same main road past Knossos. Within a very short time you're in the depths of the countryside. Move on through vines, vines and more vines, proclaiming the industry of the region (🚇 at 70km). Soon after the petrol station, fork right for Arhanes. Fork right again at the next junc-tion. Come to **Kato Arhanes** (73km 🚇) and **Arhanes** (75km 🕆🔺), with its clock tower on the right. Keep right in the one-way system, skirting round the small town. Pass a chapel and, at the square, keep to the right of the large tree. Then turn right for Vathypetro (a small signpost indicates the way). Bump down a track to the

Fresco at Knossos — the 'Priest-King'

Mullein
(Verbascum
thrapsi-
forme)

*Field
gladiolus*
(Gladiolus
segetum)

*Pome-
granate*
(Punica
granatum)

*Jerusalem
sage*
(Phlomis
fruticosa)

Minoan mansion, **Vathypetro★** (80km 🏛; Picnic 13). Notable on its south side are the wine press and ceramics kiln (16th century BC).

Once back on the main route, ignore smaller tracks going off at tangents. The surface deteriorates here, in parts becoming dirt track, but there are signs of roadworks. Turn right after you reach the first buildings of **Houdetsi** (🕇🍽) and eventually join the main asphalt road (84km). Turn left towards Iraklion (🍽 at 85km). You will be picking up speed now and, at 89km, turn right for Kasteli (🍽 not far past the turning, close to the Peza wine-makers' co-operative). At the next junction, go straight on. At **Agios Paraskies** (91km 🍽) go straight over the crossroads.

The landscape changes as you climb higher into rockier, hilly countryside with cypresses. You may find that it's reminiscent, in places, of a country lane in Tuscany. If you like, you can make a short detour to Thrapsano (turn right at 97km), one of the two villages in Crete specialising almost exclusively in pottery (the other is Margarites southeast of Rethimnon). Pass by **Apostoli**'s older church (102km) before going through the village. The road, now lined with eucalyptus, leads on towards the brown and grey hills ahead, through **Kardoulianos** (🕇) and **Kasteli** (108km 🕇🍽). Bear left for Hersonisos, at 119km go left again, and at 122km pick up the Hersonisos bypass, heading east, back to **Agios Nikolaos** (163km).

*Spiny
acanthus*
(Acanthus
spinosus)

*Cretan
ebony*
(Ebenus
cretica)

*Thorny
burnet*
(Sarcopo-
terium
spinosum)

*Shrub
tobacco*
(Nicotiana
glauca)

11 TO THE WEST

Agios Nikolaos • (Iraklion) • Rethimnon • Hania • Agios Nikolaos

404km/250mi; about 6 hours' driving; Exit A from Agios Nikolaos
On route: Walk 18

*Generally good, main-road driving. Take care when there is a solid
white line prohibiting overtaking; it's there for a reason. Even if you have
decided to stay overnight in Hania, we recommend that you head west
in the morning — otherwise the mid-day sun will dazzle you, and you
won't see a thing! Although this is a very long drive, you'll get value for
money from your car — especially if driving is shared.*

If you hire a car you'll be tempted, understandably, to
drive west. The contrast between east and west is very
marked, and this drive to Hania will impress upon you
just how large Crete is. A great deal of the route is fringed
by the sea, in its stunning shades of blue. As a backdrop
there is the awe-inspiring Mount Ida and, further west, the
White Mountains ('Levka Ori').

Leave Agios Nikolaos via Exit A. Bypass Iraklion★
(63km **ⁱⱦ🏠✕🔲⊕M**) on the national highway. You
cross two bridges, Pandanassa and Paleokastron, and
pass turnings for Agia Pelagia and Capsis Beach (🏠✕)
Soon see the turn-off to Fodele★ (88.5km **ⱦ**), El Greco's
birthplace. The orange groves there, and the Byzantine
church of Panagia, are attractions for visitors, but El
Greco's reputed birthplace is a disappointment, having
been extensively renovated and given over to tourism.

Staying on the oleander- and wild mimosa-lined road
(now referring to the map of Western Crete), pass viewpoints over the sea and the upland countryside (📷 at 106,
108 and 109km; 🔲 at 110km). Around the 125km-mark,
just before Geropotamos Bridge, the White Mountains
come into view. Even in summer they may be carrying a
mantle of snow on the peaks.

Stay on the new road towards Rethimnon and either take the second
exit if you want to visit this large
pleasant town or continue on the
national highway. **Rethimnon★**
(142km **ⁱⱦ🏠✕🔲⊕M**) has a
good beach (down right, as you
approach the centre of town).
The old harbour is a nice place
to stretch your legs. More than
any other town on Crete, this

Fodele: the Byzantine church of Panagia

45

still speaks of its medieval past, with its Ottoman and Venetian buildings. The museum is a very manageable size.

Once beyond the town (🚌 at 144km), the road rises, giving you good views back over Rethimnon's setting. Pass above the Gerani Cave★ (150km ∩), situated below the bridge of the same name. Cross the Petres River — doubtless a dry bed leading to the sea. For the next 10km (🚌 at 156km) the road runs straight along a sandy beach. If you decide to swim, take care — the currents are strong!

Driving into the 'county' of Hania, the mountains will be much more evident up to your left (📷 at 165km). Soon (169km), when Hania is within striking distance, you could turn left to Vrises (✗), where spring water flows over the roadside and yoghurt flows out of bowls. Or you could turn right into the village of Georgioupoli (▲✗) and have a swim. Pressing on to Hania (🚌 at 171km), bear in mind that photography is forbidden above the Souda Bay naval base. It's a pity, because the views are excellent. At 196km turn right to **Souda** and, at the following junction (197km), turn left. Now a pleasant old road (🚌), lined with trees, takes you into the town. A one-way system begins by the statue of a *kri-kri* (ibex). Continue by taking the right-hand fork. You are in the main street, Tzanakaki, which will lead you to the market in **Hania**★ (202km ⏸✝▲✗🚌⊕M). Perhaps this attractive town will entice you to return to Crete, make your base here, and explore the west, using *Landscapes of Western Crete*.

The Venetian harbour at Hania

Walking

We have covered a lot of ground putting these walks together, and we're sure you'll be surprised and delighted to discover so many varied landscapes in Eastern Crete. When people think of walking on Crete, they invariably imagine the White Mountains and the Samaria Gorge — Western Crete. Frankly, we're delighted that the east of the island — for all its catering to tourists — still has miles and miles of 'hidden' landscapes, just waiting for you to discover.

The 'Landscapes' series, unlike general guides or trekking guides, is built around walks and excursions that can be made *in day trips* from your home base, even if you choose not to hire a car. Accordingly, all the walks in this book are intended as day excursions from Agios Nikolaos. Obviously, there are far more walking possibilities in Eastern Crete than we have included in this book, but accessibility by *public transport* would be a problem. However we feel that the walks included present a superb cross-section of land- and seascapes.

Do consider combining some of the walks. We've indicated where routes link up on the walking maps, and the fold-out touring map shows the general location of all the walks. One word of caution: **Never try to get from one walk to another on uncharted terrain!** Only link up

walks by following paths described in these notes or by using roads or tracks; don't try to cross rough country (which might be dangerous) or private land (where you might not have the right of way). **Never** try to cross military installations or to take photographs in the area.

The people you meet are very much a part of the landscape, countryside and essence of Crete. Do greet anyone you pass or see working in a field when you are out walking. Please don't — perhaps through your natural reserve — pretend they don't exist!

There are walks in this book for everyone.

Beginners: Start on the walks graded 'easy', and
sure to check all the short and alternative walks — sor
are easy versions of the longer hikes. You need look r.
further than the picnic suggestions on pages 10-13 to finc
a large selection of easy walks — many on level ground.
Otherwise Walk 1 (Alternative 1), Short walk 5 or Walks
14, 16 or 17 might be particularly rewarding 'starter'
walks for you.

More experienced walkers: If you are accustomed to
rough terrain and are feeling fit, you should be able to
manage and enjoy all the walks in this book. Note that a
couple of the hikes will demand that you have a head for
heights as well. Take into account the season and weather
conditions. Don't attempt the more strenuous walks in
high summer; do protect yourself from the sun and carry
ample water and fruit. Always remember that storm
damage or bulldozing could make any walk described in
this book unsafe. Remember, too, always to follow the
route of the walk as we describe it. If you have not come
to one of our landmarks after a reasonable time, you must
go back to the last 'sure' point and start again.

Experts: Most of the walks that attract you will be found
in *Landscapes of Western Crete*. It's unlikely that you will
find any of the walks in the east challenge you, so relax
and simply enjoy the wonderful scenery.

Guides, waymarking, maps

While you won't need a **guide** for any walk in this
book, should you wish to walk further afield (perhaps
climb Mount Ida), we suggest you contact the Alpine Club
in Iraklion (Leof. Dikeosinis 21; telephone 081 227609).
They arrange guided trips and overnight stays.

It's always encouraging to see **waymarking** — daubs
of red paint — along the route. But, unless we specifically
advise you to follow it, don't *rely* on the waymarking. You
will also come across some part of the 'E4' network of
marked long-distance routes. These 'European Rambler
Trails' are very well waymarked with black and yellow
flags and paint marks.

The only largish-scale **map** of Crete is published by
Harms Verlag. This two-sheet map (scale 1:100 000) is
available from your local stockist, and we recommend
you buy at least the sheet covering Eastern Crete. We have
enlarged these maps to 1:50,000 and used them as a basis
for the walking maps in this book, superimposing our own

outes drawn up in the field. Since no modern 1:50 000 maps are available for reference, it is virtually *impossible* for us to make our routes *exact*. ***Important:*** In recent years there has been a sad spread of agricultural tracks — made by everyone and anyone who has olive trees. Every terrace, field, hillside or grove seems to be scarred by a motorable track. There are literally *hundreds* of them and they sprout up almost daily, making it impossible to reproduce them accurately on our maps. It is doubtless progress to the locals, but these tracks cut footpaths to bits and can make our walking notes inaccurate before the book even goes to press. We hope that the text, combined with the maps (which should give you a feel for the 'lie of the land') will help you overcome the inevitable difficulties of orientation caused by these new tracks.

Things that bite or sting

Dogs on Crete, in our experience, are full of bravado, but not vicious. They bark like fury — indeed, what would be the point of guarding livestock if they did not? — and they will approach you, seemingly full of evil intention. However, they will shy off if you continue unperturbed. '**El**-la' is a useful word to know. It means 'come here', if spoken encouragingly, or 'come off it', when said in a slightly diffident tone. Use it encouragingly with the dogs, and they'll soon go away. If you carry a walking stick, keep it out of sight and don't use it threateningly. If dogs worry you, you may like to invest in a 'Dog Dazer' — an ultrasonic device which deters threatening dogs without harming them. This is available from Sunflower Books.

In the autumn you may be startled by gunfire, but it's only **hunters** — invariably on Sundays and holidays — in pursuit of game. You'll doubtless see them dropping or throwing stones into bushes — Greek beating!

Have respect for **donkeys'** hind legs; it's highly unlikely they'll kick, but don't forget the possibility.

Snakes may be seen, and vipers have been identified on Crete, but they keep a very low profile and are not widespread. Poisonous **spiders**, called 'rogalida', do exist on the island, but it's highly unlikely you'll even catch a glimpse of one, as they are burrowers. You're more likely to see **scorpions**; they are harmless, but their sting is painful. Like spiders and snakes, they are likely to be hiding under rocks and logs in the daytime hours. So if you move a rock, etc, to sit down, just have a look under it first.

People who are allergic to bee stings should alway. carry the necessary pills. **Bees** abound in high summer, especially around water troughs and thyme bushes.

Although we've mentioned this collection of creatures, it's very doubtful indeed that you will encounter anything that would harm you.

What to take

If you're already on Crete when you find this book, and you haven't any special equipment such as a rucksack or walking boots, you can still do many of the walks — or you can buy the basic equipment at one of the sports shops in Agios Nikolaos or Iraklion. Don't attempt the more difficult walks without the proper gear. For each walk in the book, the *minimum* equipment is listed. Above all, you need thick-soled stout shoes or walking boots. *Ankle support* is advisable in your footwear — indeed *essential* on some of the walks, where the path descends steeply over loose stones. You may find the following checklist useful:

stout shoes with ankle support or walking boots	up-to-date bus timetable
long trousers, tight at the ankles	anorak (zip opening)
waterproof rain gear (outside summer months)	bandages and plasters
	extra pair of (long) socks
long-sleeved shirt (for sun protection)	knives and openers
	light cardigans (or similar)
water bottle, plastic plates, etc	antiseptic cream
tissues	whistle, torch, compass
sunhat, sunglasses, sun cream	spare bootlaces
plastic groundsheet	small rucksack
	insect repellant

Please bear in mind that we've not done *every* walk in this book under *all* conditions. We might not realise, for example, just how hot or how exposed some walks might be. Beware of the sun and the effects of dehydration. Don't be deceived by cloud cover: you can still get sunburnt, especially on the back of your neck and legs. We rely on your good judgement to modify the 'equipment' list at the start of each walk according to the season.

Where to stay

We have used Agios Nikolaos as our walking base, since the majority of people stay there when visiting Eastern Crete. Due to the size of the island, some of the walks in the east require bus changes. Although this makes the day longer, it has the advantage that you see more of the countryside. There are no organised facilities overnight stays in the mountains in Eastern Crete, but you'd like to stay in a mountain village overnight, it's worth asking for a bed for the night. The shepherd community at Katharon above Kritsa, for example, has been known to provide pleasant — although very basic — shelter for the night. Enquire about renting a bed for the night at tavernas and *cafeneions.*

If you're staying at a base other than Agios Nikolaos, the walks are still possible — just check on the bus times (see Timetables on pages 133-134), to make sure that the walks furthest away from your base are practicable.

Walkers' checklist

The following points cannot be stressed too often:
- **At any time a walk may become unsafe** due to storm damage or bulldozing. If the route is not as described in this book, and your way ahead is not secure, do not attempt to continue.
- **Never walk alone** — four is the best walking group.
- **Transport** connections at the end of a walk are vital.
- Proper **footwear** is essential.
- **Warm clothing** is needed in the mountains; even in summer, take something appropriate with you, in case you are delayed.
- **Compass, torch, whistle** weigh little, but might save your life.
- **Extra food** and drink should be taken on long walks.
- Always take a **sunhat** with you, and in summer a cover-up for your arms and legs as well.
- A **stout stick** is a help on rough terrain and to discourage the rare unfriendly dog.
- **Do not panic in an emergency.**
- Read and reread the **important note** on page 2 and the Country code on page 11, as well as guidelines on grade and equipment for each walk you plan to do.

Weather

April, May, September and October are perhaps the best months to walk on Crete. The air temperature is moderate, but the sun shines. It is possible to walk during June, July and August, however, because although it may be very hot by the coast, there's often a light breeze in the mountains. There's no doubt it's more tiring though, and great care should be taken in the sun and heat. The *meltemi* blowing in from the north tends to be a bad-tempered wind, bringing strong, hot breezes in the height of summer. These breezes stir up the dust, move the about, but don't really cool it.

During February and November it often rains. Th months of December and January are chilly and, if it rains, it may do so for two or three days at a time. However, the winter in Crete brings an incredible clarity on sunny days and some really perfect walking weather, when temperatures may be around 20°C (68°F).

It's worth remarking, too, that more often than not, when it's windy along the north coast, it's calm on the south of the island.

Greek for walkers

In the major tourist areas you hardly need to know any Greek at all but, once you are out in the countryside, a few words of the language will be helpful. Anyhow, it's nice to be able to communicate — if only a little — and people will marvel at your attempts.

Here's one way to ask directions in Greek *and understand the answers you get!* First memorise the few 'key' questions given below. Then, always follow up your key question with a **second question demanding a yes (ne) or no (ochi) answer**. (By the way, Greeks invariably raise their heads to say 'no', which looks to us like the beginning of a 'yes'. And 'ochi' (no) might be pronounced as **o**-hee, **o**-shee or even **oi**-ee.)

Following are the two most likely situations in which you may have to use some Greek. The dots (...) show where you will fill in the name of your destination. The approximate pronunciation of place names is in the Index.

■ Asking the way

The key questions

English	Approximate Greek pronunciation
Good day, greetings	**Hair**-i-tay
Hello, hi (informal)	**Yas**-sas (plural); **Yia**-soo (singular)
Please —	**Sas** pa-ra-ka-**loh** —
where is	**pou ee**-nay
the road that goes to ... ?	o **thro**-mo stoh ... ?
the footpath that goes to ... ?	ee mo-no-**pa**-ti stoh ... ?
the bus stop?	ee **sta**-ssis?
Many thanks.	Eff-hah-ree-**stoh** po-**li**.

Secondary question leading to a yes/no answer

English	Approximate Greek pronunciation
Is it here?	**Ee**-nay **etho**?
Is it there?	**Ee**-nay eh-**kee**?
Is it straight ahead?	**Ee**-nay kat-eff-**thia**?
Is it behind?	**Ee**-nay **pee**-so?
Is it to the right?	**Ee**-nay thex-**ya**?

Is it to the left?	**Ee**-nay aris-teh-**rah**?
Is it above?	**Ee**-nay eh-**pano**?
Is it below?	**Ee**-nay **kah**-to?

■ Asking a taxi driver to take you somewhere and return for you, or asking him to collect you somewhere

English	Approximate Greek pronunciation
Please —	**Sas** pa-ra-ka-**loh** —
would you take us to ... ?	tha **pah**-reh mas stoh … ?
Come and pick us up	**El**-la na mas **pah**-reh-teh
from ... (place) at ... (time)*	apo ... stees ...*

*Instead of memorising the hours of the day, simply point out on your watch the time you wish to be collected.

As you may need a taxi for some walks, why not ask your tour rep or hotel reception to find a driver who speaks English. We'd also recommend that you use an inexpensive phrase book: many give easily-understood pronunciation hints, as well as a good selection of useful phrases. It's unlikely that a map will mean anything to the people you may meet en route. Doubtless, they will ask you '**Pooh pah**-tay?' — at the same time turning a hand over in the air, questioningly. It means 'Where are you going?', and quite a good answer is 'Stah voo-**na**', which means 'to the mountains'. (We could insert here a long list of their comments on this, to which you would smile and plough on, 'Landscapes' guide in hand.)

Walk 21: at the top of the 'xiloskala' at the Samaria Gorge, with Gingilos Mountain in the background

Organisation of the walks

The 20 main walks in this book are located in the parts of Eastern Crete most easily accessible by public transport, using Agios Nikolaos as the base. We hope that even if you're staying somewhere else in the east, most will be within range. We've also included details about the famous Samaria Gorge walk in Western Crete (Walk 21), which it's possible to do from Agios Nikolaos — and one that many of you will want to undertake.

The book is set out so that you can plan walks easily — depending on how far you want to go, your abilities and equipment — and what time you are willing to get up in the morning! You might begin by considering the fold-out touring map inside the back cover of the book. Here you can see at a glance the overall terrain, the road network, and the general orientation of the walking maps in the text. Quickly flipping through the book, you'll find that there's at least one photograph for each walk.

Having selected one or two potential excursions from the map and the photographs, look over the planning information at the beginning of each walk description. Here you'll find distance/hours, grade, equipment, and how to get there and return. If the walk sounds beyond your ability or fitness, check to see if there's a shorter or alternative version given. We've tried to provide walking opportunities less demanding of agility wherever possible.

When you are on your walk, you will find that the text begins with an introduction to the overall landscape and then quickly turns to a detailed description of the route itself. Times are given for reaching certain points in the walk. Giving times is always tricky, because they depend on so many factors but, once you've done one walk, you'll be able to compare our very steady pace with your own; we hope you'll find we're in step, give or take! *Note that our times do not include any stops, so allow for them.*

Below is a key to the large-scale walking maps.

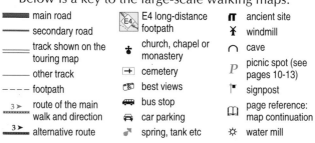

▰▰▰ main road	E4 long-distance footpath	⋔ ancient site
—— secondary road	✝ church, chapel or monastery	✗ windmill
══ track shown on the touring map	⊞ cemetery	∩ cave
—— other track	☒ best views	*P* picnic spot (see pages 10-13)
– – – footpath	🚌 bus stop	ⲓ signpost
3► route of the main walk and direction	🚗 car parking	▥ page reference: map continuation
3► alternative route	♪ spring, tank etc	☼ water mill

1 KRITSA • LATO • HAMILO

See also photographs pages 34 and 41

NB: Lato is *closed on Mondays.* Otherwise open daily from 08.30-15.00.

Distance: 8km/5mi; 2h15min

Grade: easy, with a gradual climb; the descent (200m/650ft) is stony and somewhat steeper.

Equipment: stout shoes, sunhat, picnic, water

How to get there: 🚌 to Kritsa (Timetable 3); journey time 15min

Lato

To return: 🚌 from Hamilo (not in the timetables): departs 15.00 *weekdays only;* journey time 10min

Alternative walks

1 Kritsa — Lato — Kritsa (7-8km/4.5-5mi; 2h15min). 🚌 as above to/from Kritsa or 🚗: park in the free car park on the right, just before the one-way system enters the main part of Kritsa village. This will take the same amount of time, but it's an easier walk, and there are many more buses from Kritsa (see Timetable 3). Equipment as above. Follow the main walk to Lato, then return along the asphalt road, perhaps making a diversion to Panagia Kera, the church shown on page 41 (see map).

2 Kritsa — Tapes — Kritsa (11.5km/7mi; 4h). Moderate ascents/descents of about 200m/650ft; equipment as main walk; access as Alternative walk 1. Follow the main walk to the 40min-point (the rough aggregate road). Here carry on straight uphill, passing a breeze-block and concrete building with double gates (on the left; 50min). Take the first right fork after this farm building and ignore a track going off to the right almost immediately. Pass a fenced-off, large breeze-block building up to the right (1h). (There may be dogs around here.) A few minutes later, pass through a wire gate — closing it behind you. Continue along the track, keeping the wire fence on the left and moving gradually uphill. Very shortly after the wire gate, the track narrows to a path. Disregarding a small building and a gateway off to the left, carry on uphill on an old donkey trail, keeping the fencing to your left. Head left over three horizontal rocks (1h15min) and continue along the path; there is a stone wall on the left. The path starts to run high up (but not vertiginously so) along the right-hand side of the river valley, then goes gently downhill. At some point along here you will notice the houses of Tapes up ahead of you in the distance. Keep your goal in mind, in case you encounter any route-finding problems from here on. The path goes through a wire mesh gate, beyond which a grassy track develops (1h35min). You're now down on the level of the river bed, walking on the flat through olive trees. Stay on the right-hand side of the river, which becomes a stream bed. Four or five minutes later pass through another gate; within a few paces you're back on the stream bed, crossing over to the other side. Then you re-cross the stream bed once more, keeping to the wide and easy grassy track. Before long, look left to see where to cross the stream bed again: there's an old gnarled olive tree straight ahead and one either side of the path. A quite well-defined, but very narrow path leads you through an olive grove. Continue diagonally uphill, looking for a small water trough, and keep to the right of it as you ascend. From here you can see the path ahead — a narrow earthen path strewn with stones. From this point it winds steeply uphill. Having seen the houses of Tapes earlier, you'll know which way you're heading. When you reach the

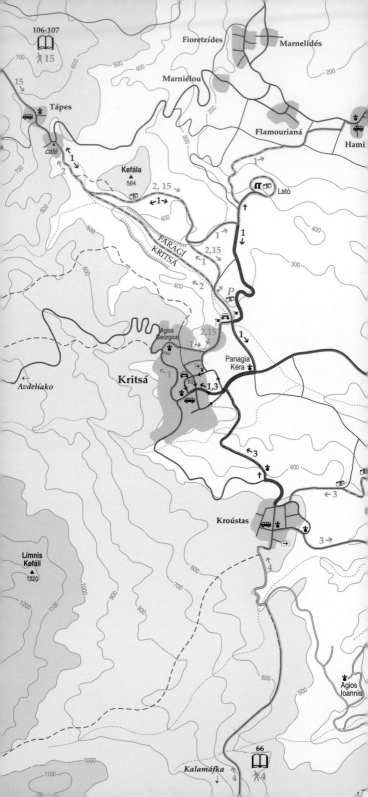

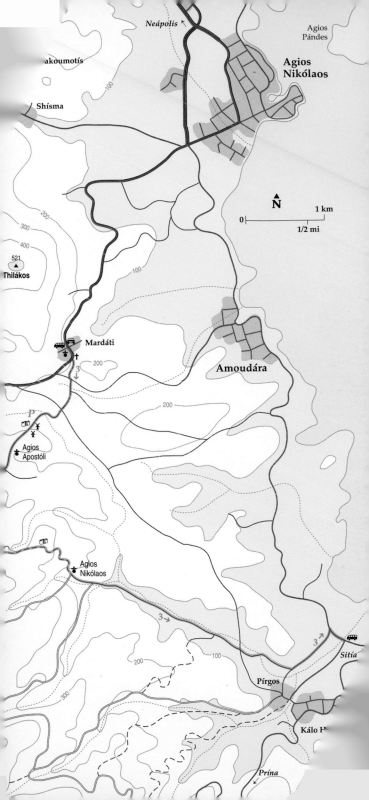

outskirts of the hamlet (1h55min), curve left on old concrete trail
two minutes later, come to a *cafeneion* with painted spiral staircase (2
From here retrace your steps to return to Kritsa (4h). The route
described in Walk 15, starting at the 4h10min-point.

H ere's a good introduction to the hills around Agios
Nikolaos: after each range yet another summit comes
into view and then fades into the distance. This is also a
pleasant way to visit the ancient Dorian site at Lato,
avoiding the asphalt road.

Either leave the car in the car park (Alternative walks)
or take the bus to where it turns round in **Kritsa**. Whichever you choose to do, **start out** by walking uphill into
the village along the main street, passing the big church
of Agios Ioannis on your right, opposite a *cafeneion* and
taxi rank. At the fork at the top of the road turn right (left
goes to Kroustas) and continue along this shop-lined road,
passing a small square filled with café tables and chairs.
When you come to a three-way fork, take the middle
route — a small concreted village road. (The route to the
left is signposted to Katharon; to the right are steps leading
downhill.) At the end of the road, keep right downhill at
a telegraph pole. Ignore any turnings left or right. You will
arrive at the large church of **Agios Georgios**. Walk across
the front of it and bend down to the right just after it, on
concrete steps. The concrete gives way to cobbles; this
was an old donkey trail.

Very soon you're at the edge of the village with views
to the Dikti range in the distance. At the bottom of the
cobbled steps, turn right and head diagonally across a
track (which may become an asphalt road), to pick up a
donkey trail on the far side. This takes you steeply downhill (take care, it's slithery!). The cobbles become a rough
track which takes you past a water trough and onto a
concrete village road. At the bottom of this road, go left
on the asphalt road to Lato. Follow this road round, past
a sign to Lato, and cross over an old bridge (**20min**). Turn
left immediately after the bridge on a rough track heading
towards the Kritsa Gorge (SIGNPOSTED 'TO THE GORGE').

About 400m/yds along, as you pass two CONCRETED
CISTERNS and an orange water pump on the right (**25min**),
you can make a diversion down into the Kritsa Gorge (see
Walk 2) by turning left. Otherwise, turn right uphill on a
rough track, to continue to Lato. Four to five minutes from
this junction, on the brow of the hill, look for a donkey
ail going up to the left and follow it. Watch out, a short
y along (**35min**), when you are on level ground again,

.nd follow the trail carefully as it makes a wide bend up
o the left; it's easy to miss this bend, as it looks as if a path
goes straight ahead at this point. The donkey trail runs
alongside a wall and then continues with walls either
side. Five minutes later (**40min**) the donkey trail peters
out at a rough aggregate road. Here turn right for Lato (or
continue straight ahead to Tapes, if you are doing
Alternative walk 2).

Walk for 20 minutes and, when you meet the asphalt
road, turn left. In five minutes pass a small trail off left,
opposite a SHRINE. You will be taking this on the way down
to Hamilo, but for now keep straight on up the road to the
Lato SITE (**1h15min**). The Dorians chose a delightful
setting, with wonderful views over almond and olive trees
down to their harbour at Agios Nikolaos and the splendid
Mirabello Gulf.

Once you've rambled round the site, go back to where
you came in and walk back down the asphalt road to the
shrine. Then take the path opposite it. This very stony
donkey trail descends in great steps beside a shrub-
clothed ravine, which is quite unexpected and makes a
picturesque contrast to the Lasithi mountains beyond. Six
minutes after turning onto this trail, it divides. You can
either go straight on or take the lower trail, which just cuts
off the corner. There are some red arrows here.

Thirty minutes from Lato (**1h45min**), you meet a track.
Turn right along it and then, almost immediately, take
another track to the right (by some transformers). After five
minutes, fork left. In another five minutes, at another fork,
branch off right. You're on the fertile plain of Lakonia,
which is covered with olive trees. Disregard a turning to
the right (**2h**). Two minutes later (**2h02min**) you've almost
come to the main road; take the track to the right, just
before the road, by a white stone building. In another two
minutes, turn left at a T-junction. Five minutes more and
you're on the main Lakonia road. Turn right and come
into **Hamilo**, where you'll doubtless be pleased to see two
tavernas. The BUS STOP is opposite the church (**2h15min**).

2 KRITSA GORGE

See map pages 56-57   **Distance:** 9km/5.6mi; 3h55min
Grade: moderate, with climbs and descents of about 280m/900ft.
Agility is required for scrambling and jumping down boulders.
Equipment: stout shoes or boots, sun hat, water, picnic
How to get there and return: 🚌 to/from Kritsa (Timetable 3); journey
time 15min, or 🚗 to/from Kritsa. You can park in the free car park on
the right, just before the one-way system enters the main part of Kritsa.
But our timings start on the Lato road: take the right turn to Lato as you
arrive at Kritsa, by a small church; drive for a minute or so and park just
before a small bridge, beyond which there is a sign for Lato (straight on)
and the Kritsa Gorge (left).

A very accessible, small, but splendid gorge makes
Kritsa an excellent hub not only for shopping, site-
visiting, and hill-village exploring, but for walking off the
beaten track as well.

To **start the walk** from the BUS STOP OR CAR PARK in
Kritsa, follow Walk 1 to the 20min-point (page 58). Alternatively, if you park by the BRIDGE (where our timings
start), head left on a rough track immediately past the
bridge. There is a road sign indicating 'Lato' to the right
here, and a hand-painted sign on the left, indicating your
route 'TO THE GORGE'. You can see the gorge immediately,
straight ahead. About 400m/yds off the road (**5min**),
where there are two CONCRETED CISTERNS and an orange
water pump on the right, turn left down towards the gorge
(ARROW WAYMARK). In a minute you're amongst big, smooth
boulders and stones — and a good amount of shade.

The route heads over to the left bank for a short stretch
and through a WAYMARKED GATE. Back on the river bed
(**10min**), you come to a large ROCK-FALL. At first glance, it
seems to bar your route (and the blue waymarking has
just deserted you). But it's possible to scramble over this,
on the right-hand side. Then you arrive at what looks like
another dead-end — a large SCREE-FALL to the left and a
fenced-off area ahead to the right. But go through the
GATEWAY IN THE FENCING and you will see the gorge off to
the right. (In case the fencing moves, note that there is a
large cairn on the left at this point.) Now the gorge walls
rear up beside you, and it's refreshingly cool.

Before long (**20min**) the gorge is at its narrowest. After
you have passed through the gorge, the river bed opens
out slightly (**35min**). When you reach a T-junction of
sorts, head round to the right. If a NETTING FENCE running
across the river bed bars the way (**1h05min**), go up and
over to the left, as you do need to carry straight on in the
river bed. At another NETTING FENCE across a narrower
section of river bed (**1h20min**), squeeze underneath.

There's a CAIRN the other side of it to encourage you! Following the bends of the river bed, within 10min you come to another FENCE with a CAIRN beyond it (**1h30min**).

Keep looking over to the right, and you will notice a path halfway up the hillside (**2h**), running along beneath the rock face; it's your return route to Kritsa. Shortly after spotting that path, you may have to negotiate a fallen tree. Just afterwards, as you approach a FENCE, look again off to the right, where you may notice a CAIRN, and head off the river bed here: unlatch the MAKESHIFT GATE up on the right-hand side of the river bed and walk through on a grassy track. (This is your return route: you will come back through this gate and continue up above the river bed.)

Five minutes later you catch a glimpse of Tapes up ahead and then pass through another GATE (**2h10min**). Shortly afterwards, the now-stony track leads up left from the stream bed. Within a few minutes it crosses the stream bed again, Half a minute later, cross the stream bed and go up into an olive grove on your left. Continue diagonally uphill, looking for a small WATER TROUGH (**2h15min**). Pass slightly to the right of this trough; from here you can

see your route ahead — a small earthen path, strewn with stones. From here it winds steeply uphill. (Having seen the houses of Tapes earlier, you will know which way you are heading.) It's a good five- to eight-minute climb to the outskirts of **Tapes**. Curve left on old concrete track and, two minutes later, reach a *cafeneion* with a painted metal spiral staircase (**2h25min**).

You can either go back via the gorge or, for easier walking, pick up the notes for Walk 15 at the 4h10min-point (page 107). Our timings end at the BRIDGE ON THE LATO ROAD outside **Kritsa** (**3h55min**).

In the gorge

3 MARDATI • KROUSTAS • KALO HORIO

See map pages 56-57; see also photographs pages 13, 39
Distance: 13km/8mi; 4h10min
Grade: moderate-strenuous; ascent of over 300m/1000ft and a long descent of about 500m/1500ft. Plenty of shade en route
Equipment: stout shoes, sunhat, picnic, water, swimwear
How to get there: 🚐 to Mardati (Kritsa bus, Timetable 3); journey time less than 10min
To return: 🚐 from Kalo Horio (Timetables 5, 6, 8); journey time 20min
Short walk: Mardati to Kroustas (4km/2.5mi; 1h 30min). Moderate ascent of 300m/ 1000ft. Equipment as above, except for swimwear. Return from Kroustas (not in the timetables): buses depart 13.30, 14.45, 17.00, 17.45 (Mon-Sat); 15.00 (Sun). Follow the main walk to Kroustas.
Alternative walk: Mardati — Kroustas — Kritsa (8km/5mi; 2h 35min). Moderate climb of 300m/ 1000ft and descent of 200m/650ft. Equipment as main walk, except swimwear. Access as main walk; return by bus from Kritsa (Timetable 3); journey time 15min. Or

🚗: park at Mardati or Kritsa, and link up with the Kritsa bus (Timetable 3). To circle back to Kritsa instead of going to Kalo Horio, turn right onto the main road in Kroustas and walk downhill towards Kritsa. In about 10 minutes, just before a shrine on the right, turn right downhill on a fairly steep old donkey trail. You soon see a small concrete-roofed shelter on your left and pass a small chapel on the right. Keep descending (visually to the right of the end of the village of Kritsa in the distance). After 40 minutes of descent, when you meet a track, curve left to continue on the donkey trail. This route is narrow and rough in parts and will be scratchy in spring. Ten minutes later, turn left on a track which soon crosses a watercourse (likely to be dry in summer). Head uphill and, at the next junction, go right towards Kritsa. At the next junction, go right and cross a bridge. You meet the main road near the exit from Kritsa's one-way system (55min from Kroustas). Follow it to the centre (15 minutes; 2h35min).

Not far from Agios Nikolaos, this is a fairly tough outing with pleasant rewards and a choice of places to end the walk. A modicum of effort will take you via deep countryside and the enchanting village of Kroustas, to a sandy beach or, if you do the Alternative walk, almost in a circle to Kritsa.

Get off the bus (or park) by the few houses of **Mardati**. **Start out** by continuing along the road towards Kritsa. Pass a SHRINE on the left and then turn left down a track (**5min**). It meanders through olive groves and pasture land. Early in the season you may well have the company of donkeys and goats grazing nonchalantly on either side of you. Two minutes along, come to a T-junction: turn left

62

and then immediately right, now following a sandy track. Almost at once, take the fork to the right. Go straight over a crossing track (**12min**) and, a minute later, pass evidence of building on your right. Cross over to the far side of the river bed on your left, and take the first track on the left, which leads uphill. After two minutes you'll have a lovely view of Kritsa on your right (Picnic 2). Two minutes further uphill are some OLD MILLS, now used to store grain. Ahead is the church of **Agios Apostoli**. Carry straight on up the track for another minute, then take the right-hand fork, up a hill. Go straight over another crossing track (**30min**). After a few minutes puffing up what is now a very steep trail through an abundance of wild flowers in spring, you get a good view of the river bed and a glimpse of Agios Nikolaos and Mirabello Bay.

Soon the trail becomes a path and, past a WATER TROUGH, just as the way bends to the right, you can take a break under a shady tree and enjoy views back to Agios Nikolaos. Then continue on the very narrow, stony and winding path. Soon you come to terraced plots, dotted with almond trees. The landscape is a maze of rocks.

When the path meets a track (**55min**), turn left; another view of Kritsa is to the right. Beyond and to the right, in the distance, lies the village of Tapes (Walk 15). Having followed the wide track round the top of the hill, you can see over to the other side (**1h**). Here's your first glimpse of your destination, Kalo Horio, and the beautiful hills beyond it. When the track splits, keep right and uphill. Round another bend, the church at Kroustas comes into view (**1h10min**). When you come to a fork, keep left. Soon you're in the back streets of the enchanting village of **Kroustas** (**1h22min**). Wend your way towards the centre, walk up to a vine-covered *cafeneion* and take the turning left just beyond it. If you're thirsty, and all the tavernas and *cafeneions* look shut, just wait a minute. Doubtless someone will see you and open up. Stay on the wider streets until you meet the main asphalt road between Kroustas and Kritsa. Turn left on this road to continue the walk. (*The Alternative walk turns right here towards Kritsa; Walk 4 also ends on this road.*)

Just before the POST BOX on the wall and a TELEPHONE KIOSK on the corner, take a left turn off this main street. Then take your first right, then your first left (both are T-junctions). Then keep hard right again, where there is a small CHURCH on your left. Now you should be heading south out of Kroustas on a wide downhill path (**1h45min**).

It curves round through plots, and then the landscape changes quite noticeably. As you leave, look back at Kroustas, sheltering behind a huge buttress of rock. The path is now a concrete track. Trees are few and far between; there is a feeling of wide open spaciousness. After five minutes, keep left on the concrete track. Almost immediately there is a WINNOWING CIRCLE on your right. Soon the track becomes earthen underfoot. In another five minutes, the track goes right, but there is still an old path straight ahead: you can take this path (which will rejoin the track), or stay on the track which is easier walking. About 20 minutes from leaving Kroustas (**2h05min**), the track curves sharp left. Here, at the left-hand bend, take a path off to the right. It is waymarked with red dots and a cairn. This old cobbled path leads down into a small GORGE. Note: this path is very narrow and scattered with loose stones; take care and watch your step. You soon cross over the largish stones in the river bed, then head up the other side. On climbing the hillside opposite, you will see a couple of CAVES.

Cross the brow of the hill (**2h30min**). Spectacular views await you: first over Agios Nikolaos and then, a little further on, over Kalo Horio, nestling in a basin surrounded by hills, open on one side to the sea. You may notice the occasional blob of red paint on rocks — reassurance that this steep downhill path is the right one. When the path next forks (**3h10min**), go left and head down towards some stone walls (red arrow waymark). One minute later pass a small church called **Agios Nikolaos**. Just beyond it your way becomes a track. Keep straight on. In 10 minutes pass a smallholding on the left. Cross an old stream bed, and the landscape opens up in front of you. Keep right, on the wide track. The river bed runs alongside you on the left.

Fifteen minutes later, take the left-hand fork, staying beside the river bed. Keep on this track. Five minutes later, ignore two turnings to the left, but two minutes later go left. Cross the river bed and head below an ugly concrete building (*do not* go over the river bed until you can see this building). If in doubt, head for the sea! The track meets the main road at **Kalo Horio** (**4h05min**). Turn right, cross the bridge, and find the BUS STOP on the far side of the road, by a taverna (**4h10min**). If you fancy a swim, go under the bridge and to the right. Walk in the river bed, taking the left-hand fork. When you come to some greenhouses, turn right for the beach (20min; photograph page 39).

4 KALAMAFKA TO KROUSTAS

Distance: 11km/7mi; 3h20min

Grade: straightforward — along track most of the way; ascents/descents of about 200m/650ft

Equipment: stout shoes, sunhat, picnic, water

How to get there: 🚌 to Kalamafka (Males bus; not in the timetables): departs Agios Nikolaos 06.00, 14.00 *Mon-Fri only;* journey time 40min
To return: 🚌 from Kroustas (not in the timetables): departs 10.45, 13.30, 14.45, 17.00, 17.30 (Mon-Sat); 15.00 (Sun); journey time 30min

This undemanding country ramble starts and ends in attractive villages and takes us through cultivated hillsides and pastures. The bus journey to Kalamafka is an experience in itself, as it's a school run, and they tend to use the older buses. Do take time to wander up into Kalamafka and, if you've got enough energy, look round the back streets of Kroustas, too — this is real Greece.

The bus stops in the middle of **Kalamafka. Start out** by walking on through the village and take the right-hand fork when the road splits. The left fork leads to Ierapetra. The road we are on skirts the side of Kalamafka. Ignore a concrete track off to the right, just before the road bends to the left. Leave the main road just after a bridge, by turning right on a concrete track (**10min**) which becomes a rough track and leads to **Kefalavrisi**, the head of a spring (**15min**). It's a nice cool place to sit for a moment or enjoy Picnic 7. Cross the stream bed, staying on the track. Almost immediately, at a crossing track, turn left.

Now on the other side of the dry watercourse, the track starts to climb (**30min**). Four minutes later, disregard a track going off to the right. A small light-coloured building becomes visible far ahead (**45min**). Ignore a track going back off to the left (**1h**). The way flattens out; stay on the main route — there are VINEYARDS ahead and to the left of the track. In a couple of minutes follow the track left round the end of a vineyard and then go right (there is an E4 WAYMARK on the tree here), rather than complete the circuit of the vineyard. Soon the track starts to descend through pine trees. Turn left at a crossing track (**1h20min**; an E4 WAYMARK points to the right here). In a couple of minutes, when the way forks again, go right uphill, to skirt

Walking the easy track from Kalamafka to Kroustas

more agricultural land. At the next fork, keep left downhill. On a wide bend to the left (**1h30min**), leave the track briefly — walking off to the right for a lovely view over Kalo Horio and the north coast.

Rounding another bend in the track (**1h45min**), Agios Nikolaos comes into view ahead. Keep right a minute later, ignoring a track to the left. Just after the track passes an ANIMAL SHELTER on the right (**2h30min**), keep ahead, ignoring a track to the left. Then ignore the next small track downhill to the left. At the point where there is FENCING on the right and a low WALL on the left of the track (**2h 35min**), fork left downhill on a path, towards the country road to Prina. Just after the top of the path you have a good view of Kroustas. The stony path crosses a stretch of flatter olive groves, where the path is faint. Look for the path carrying on downhill, and *don't* be misled into striking off right on a track here. The last section is clearly an old donkey trail, and it meets the road at a bridge. Go left over the BRIDGE (**3h 10min**) and head uphill into **Kroustas**. You pass the church on your right at the start of the village. The bus from Kritsa comes in where the road opens out between the houses. It turns round here and leaves from beside the kiosk — next to a *cafeneion* (**3h20min**).

Alternatively, you can walk on to Kritsa: use the notes for Alternative walk 3 on page 62.

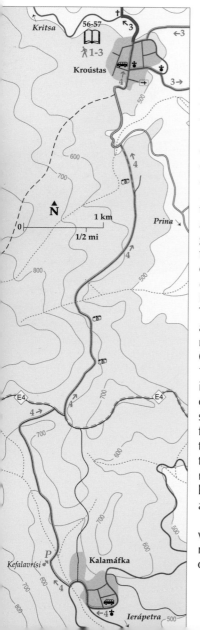

5 ROUND AGIOS IOANNIS POINT

Photograph: ruined mills near Vrouhas; see also photographs pages 1 and 74
See map pages 70-71
Distance: 11km/7mi; 3h30min

Grade: quite easy, after a steep ascent at the start; possibility of vertigo on the narrow coastal path. Total ascents/descents about 300m/1000ft.

Equipment: stout shoes, sunhat, picnic, water, long trousers, swimwear

How to get there and return: 🚍 to/from Plaka (Timetable 7); journey time 40min. Or by 🚗: park in Plaka.

Short walk: Agios Ioannis Point from near Vrouhas (7km/4.5mi; 2h15min). Easy, but possibility of vertigo on the narrow coastal path. Equipment as above; access by 🚗 to/from Vrouhas: park by the ruined mills and small church on the road from Plaka to Vrouhas (the 40min-point in the main walk). Then follow the main walk to the 2h55min-point — when you will arrive back at your car. A few of the mills are shown in this photograph, which was taken from near Vrouhas.

It's sea, sea and more sea on this walk. It glistens and sparkles tantalisingly all around you. As you round Agios Ioannis Point on a high coastal path, you'll have breathtaking views out over 'big' and 'little' Spinalonga, as well as Kolokithia — all set like precious stones in a sea which changes from pale aquamarine to the deepest sapphire blue.

From the BUS STOP at **Plaka**, **start out** by walking north along the road, with the beach on your right. When the beach comes to an end and the road curves round to the left, you'll see a track heading off to the right. Follow it and, within a couple of minutes, ignore a path going towards the sea to the right of three low domed buildings and a path going straight ahead. Take the rough agricultural track going left, steeply up the hillside. When you reach the main road to Vrouhas (**25min**), climb over the crash barrier (noticing where you do so, as it is harder to find on your return descent). Now turn right and climb as far as the first hairpin bend. At about the halfway point in the hairpin turn, climb another path leading right, up the hillside. Rejoining the road in five minutes, turn right; then keep to the road for five minutes more. You approach some old WINDMILLS and a small CHURCH (**40min**). *(This is the starting point for the Short walk and Picnic 4.)*

Here take a concrete track off to the right. After a few minutes, leave the track and walk a short way off the

67

route, seawards. You'll have wonderful views down over Spinalonga and back to Plaka (Picnic 4). Return to the concrete track but, about 250m/yds past a small CHURCH (**1h**), *search out* your ongoing path off to the right (just before the track bends to the left). It is hard to see the start of this path, except in high summer, as bushes have grown up over the stone wall. But there *is* a cairn here. Once you find it, the path is obvious — although you might wish you'd taken secateurs with you. The path veers to the left and soon has stone walls on either side of it, and the sea is down to the right. A track can be seen running beside the sea; soon it will climb to intercept this path.

After a short while, there's only a wall on the left. On the right there are splendid views out over tiny Kolokithia ('Bird') Island and, further to the right, over 'big' Spinalonga (photograph below) and the causeway at Olous. You pass by a small CAVE down the hill on the right and a large one up to the left (**1h15min**). A little way past here, there is a slight danger of vertigo, although the land slopes, rather than drops, down to the sea. It is not a sheer drop, but in places the sea side of the path is unprotected.

If you see what looks like another path veering off uphill, stay on the overgrown path leading straight ahead (**1h20min**). Twenty minutes later the path meets the track you spotted earlier (**1h40min**). Join the track and round a gully; then curve round a second little gully. Keep on the main track, which curves left round the hillside. Stay on the track until it bends to the right (**1h50min**); here you go left, heading west into the olive grove. (Or stay on the

track all the way to the church of Agios Ioannis out on the headland and then return to this right-hand bend and head west into the olive grove.) Cross the olive grove diagonally, to some wire mesh netting (at the time of writing). Take the path just above the top end of the fence; after some 50m/yds the path curves west up the hill. In a couple of minutes there are walls on both sides of the path, as you approach the ruins of **Katos**, a hamlet built across the hillside. Pass through another band of olive trees. The path curves left through the old houses. Continue uphill and then, when you meet a cobbled track, turn left (**2h10min**). The sea will be on your left now. Five minutes along the track, find a water trough and a large WATER TANK, where you may see groups of animals drinking. Keep straight on past this watering place; ignore a track to the right.

Turn left on another track (**2h30min**) and stay on it (disregarding a path forking off left and a couple of tracks going off to the right). When you rejoin the main concrete track (**2h40min**), follow it to the left. You'll pass the point where you initially turned off this track to go down to the sea. Soon, off to the right, you can see the village of Loumas on a hill in the distance and then Vrouhas comes into view down to the right (**2h45min**).

Ten minutes later you're back on the main road (**2h 55min**). The Short walk ends here; the main walk turns left on the road. In five minutes go left on the path which drops down to meet the road — halfway round the hairpin bend. Walk on and then take the track back down into

Plaka (**3h30min**). There is plenty of time for a swim in the beautiful clear water off the shore at Plaka before catching a bus. The BUS STOP is at the south (Elounda) side of the village, opposite a track.

Picnic 4 and Walk 5: from the coastal path, 'little' Spinalonga floats on the aquamarine sea, just north of the larger island of the same name.

6 ELOUNDA • PINES • HAVGAS • PLAKA

See also photographs pages 1 and 68-69

Distance: 11km/7mi; 3h20min

Grade: fairly strenuous, with a steep initial ascent of 350m/1150ft lasting about 40 minutes. The corresponding descent is gradual, but you must be surefooted.

Equipment: stout shoes, sunhat, picnic, water, long trousers, swimwear

How to get there: 🚌 to Elounda (Timetables 2, 7); journey time 20min; or 🚗
To return: 🚌 from Plaka (Timetable 7) — back to your car or to Agios Nikolaos (journey time 40min)

Short walk: Kato Pines — Elounda (2.5km/ 1.5mi; 45min). This pleasant, undemanding leg-stretch would be a perfect 'constitutional' on what you might want to make a 'lazy' day. Take a bus to Elounda (Timetables 2, 7) and from there a five minute taxi journey to Kato Pines. Ask to be dropped off by the first *cafeneion,* on the left-hand side of the main road. Take the path opposite the *cafeneion* and head up to the right on a donkey trail. After one minute you are at a crossroads, with one working windmill on your left and two sail-less mills on the right. Go straight across and walk downhill to a donkey trail, with stone walls coming in from the right (3min). Continue on this trail; from here it's an easy downhill walk. Along your route, you'll see several round stone enclosures used by the local people for their threshing. You may be lucky enough to see them working (depending on the time of year); it's a long way from our world of combine harvesters. At the outset there are good views down over Elounda. The road crosses your route in several minutes, but continue straight over it to rejoin the trail. Pass a small church on your right, cross the road, and then pass another, newer church on the left (14min). Ignore the tarmac road coming in from the left and take the fork to the right, into the village of Pano Elounda. When you are in Pano Elounda, keep straight down the narrow path ahead. (Some building work is going on here, so you may have to improvise your route.) Then go down some wide shallow concrete steps, which curve first to the left and then to the right. Turn left and carry on through the village, past a *cafeneion.* When you meet a concrete track crossing the route, follow it to the left and go under a bridge. The road is above you here (30min). Soon after the bridge you come to the road (35min). Turn

70

Vlihádia

Agios Geórgios

Skiniás

←Váltos

⚓ Houdrováli

701
▲
Kadistó

600

6

6

500

600

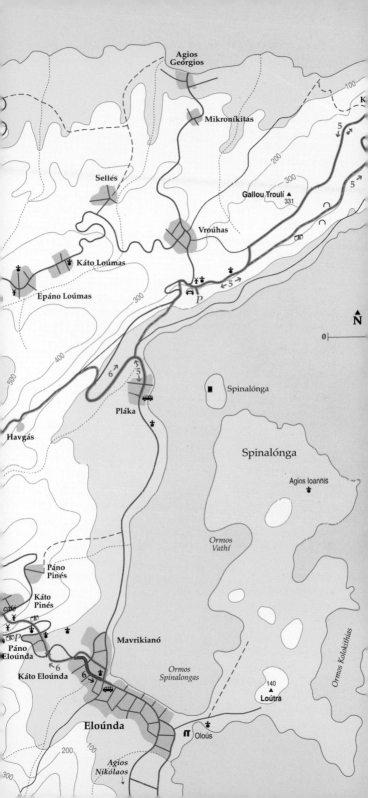

right by the sign for Pano Elounda. Follow the road through Kato Elounda and on into Elounda itself, where you will emerge by the church.

Within minutes of leaving the middle of Elounda and the trappings of tourism, you're out in the country, following in the footsteps of Cretan folk who have used the donkey trails for years. While this isn't a very long walk, it does involve some steep climbing. Needless to say, you'll be compensated by the joy of discovering some lovely views that the postcards never quite capture. And you will end up at one of our favourite swimming spots.

It's unlikely that this will be your only visit to Elounda, but anyway do make sure you sit on the right-hand side of the bus on your way there — the views are magnificent. Get off the bus and **start the walk** in the centre of **Elounda**. Walk towards the CLOCK TOWER and turn right immediately beyond it. Take the first turning left, by the Ferryman's Music Bar. This was the original donkey trail away from the coast. It's now concreted, but it becomes more authentic as you draw away from the sea.

The trail forks either side of a telephone pole (**6min**); go right. Within a few metres/yards the trail is stone-walled on both sides. When the trail meets a road where there is a sign to Mavrikiano (**8min**), cross straight over. The surface becomes cobbled. In three minutes the trail splits; take the left-hand (wider) fork. Very shortly come to the main road to Kato Pines; cross it diagonally to continue on up the trail, which is again concreted and bordered by stone walls. A CHURCH stands out (**10min**), set up on the right.

Stay on the trail until you come to a small BRIDGE carrying the Kato Pines road over the trail. Almost at once, past the bridge, turn up a concrete path to the right, into the very pretty village of **Pano Elounda** (**15min**), with its lovely old wooden doors, balconies, bougainvillea and vines. Walk through the village and, just past two *cafeneions* (one either side of you), turn right. Pass another *cafeneion;* then, as the route bends downhill, look up left and go up the wide shallow concrete steps that curve round and uphill. At the top go straight ahead, across an open area, to rejoin the path — now bordered by stone walls. There is a CHURCH on the right.

When you come out onto the road (**30min**), cross it and go up the donkey trail opposite (which is concreted at the start). Two minutes uphill there is a small CHURCH and some olive trees offering welcoming shade and good

Above: Detail of the stonework on the Venetian fortress on Spina-longa Island, built in 1579. Right: windmill on the crest between Pano Elounda and Kato Pines.

views over Elounda — a nice picnic spot (Picnic 5). Three minutes further on, cross the road again and take the donkey trail directly opposite. It heads round to the right initially, next to the road.

Turn left on a much wider track (**40min**) and, after a minute or two, you will reach the top of a crest, where there is a working WINDMILL on your right (see above) and two sail-less mills on your left. Their owner is often about and happy to show off the inside of one of the mills for a small financial token. As the trail ends near these mills, carry on down the concrete track just to your left. After two minutes cross over the road and continue on the concrete track opposite. You'll pass the few houses of **Kato Pines**, and you may see some people at work in the fields, perhaps threshing or winnowing. Keep straight on.

Before long the concrete gives way to a cobbled path (**1h**), and you start to climb. Stay on the main route until the first turning right (**1h15min**), take it and then follow the way as it curves round to the left. After two minutes, keep going round to the right, and then curve round to the left. Keep right and then left, as the path curves up the hillside. Then keep left at a fork (there are stone walls on both sides of the ongoing path). At last, come to the road (**1h25min**). Join it and turn right.

In about five minutes' walking along the road, there is a sign indicating a double bend ahead. About 40m/yds past this sign, on the left-hand side of the road, there's a donkey trail set off by stone walls. Climb up here and, after a minute, turn left at a fork. Shortly after this, come to another fork and head right.

Then start to descend. When you meet a crossing track (**1h45min**), turn left along it. Two minutes later, where the stone wall on the right curves round, turn right on a concreted track. Follow it to descend into the valley. At the bottom, turn left. The track soon becomes a path and then curves uphill to the right; it quickly begins to climb. In a few more minutes you can rest in the shade of a large holly oak.

Set off again and, at the next fork, go left (slightly downhill). Then quite quickly, climb again — up a steep incline. Still climbing, you'll pass under another shady tree. Now there's wire mesh on your left and, although clearly defined, the path is hedged in by lots of shrubbery, much of it prickly and thorny. (Beware scratched legs, if you're not wearing long trousers.) The path curves round to the right and levels out somewhat. Turn left and reach a wide track in half a minute (**2h15min**).

Head right on this track. Within a few minutes, you will glimpse the tail of Spinalonga Island, surrounded by a vivid blue sea — the setting framed by the mountains ahead. Soon (**2h30min**) you can look down to the right, for an excellent view of the gorge and another wonderful sea vista beyond it. Ahead, the hamlet of Havgas completes the tableau, adding a human scale to this impressive landscape.

Pass by **Havgas** (**2h40min**) and keep downhill on the track. We suggest you stay on this new track; it takes slightly longer than looking for and following old bits of donkey trail which, although more direct, are very overgrown and somewhat ruined by the track. When the track joins an asphalt road (**2h50min**), turn right and follow the road down to **Plaka**. The BUS STOP is on the far side of the village, opposite the bus shelter (**3h20min**).

The crystal-clear sea at Plaka

7 VASILIKI TO EPISKOPI

See map pages 76-77; see also photographs pages 25 and 83

Distance: 12km/7.5mi; 3h55min

Grade: moderate, with a climb and descent of about 350m/1150ft; a straightforward walk along tracks; very little shade.

Equipment: stout shoes, sunhat, picnic, water

How to get there: 🚌 to the Vasiliki turn-off (Ierapetra bus, Timetable 5); journey time 35min. Or 🚗 to Vasiliki

To return: 🚌 from Episkopi (Timetable 5; departs Episkopi 10-15 minutes after leaving Ierapetra); journey time 45min to Agios Nikolaos, 10min back to the Vasiliki turn-off

This moderate ramble will take you through some lovely open countryside, with views stretching from the sea in the north to the sea in the south, and you will have a gradual climb over the hills facing the splendid Thripti Mountains, settings for Walks 8, 9 and 10. The route takes you past an old shepherd community, and the last section is along a wide and easy track.

The bus stop for Vasiliki comes up soon after the road turns south towards Ierapetra. Look out for a deep gorge on the left and a sign for Monastiraki just before the stop. (You will doubtless marvel at the gorge; Walk 8 brings you down here from behind it — hard to believe?)

Start the walk from the BUS STOP by following the Vasiliki road up to the right. Pass a sign to an archaeological site off to the left (**2min**). Entering **Vasiliki** (**15min**), pass the sign for the village and keep straight ahead. After curving to the left, turn right into the main street. Pass the first narrow turn-off to the left, but then take the next left (there is an E4 WAYMARK here) — a wider road that leads up a slope. Along here, take the third turn-off to the left, by a telephone pole, just at the top end of the village.

As it leaves Vasiliki, this path turns into a wider track, from where you'll have good views of the farmlands below, spread with a mass of greenhouses gleaming under the sun. In spring the hills ahead will be covered with mauvy-pink clover — Cretan ebony. Later in the season, there will be bright yellow gorse everywhere. When the many flowers die, they are replaced by a haze of heather, and Cretan ebony wears a furry hat for autumn.

When the track divides (**25min**), go left and, a minute later, ignore another track coming in from the left. Five minutes later the track divides again (there is a stone building on the left here; **30min**). Ignore the turning left. In three minutes you'll pass by a good place for a picnic (Picnic 3). Follow the E4 WAYMARKS uphill. You will have

N

0   1 km

1/2 mi

Konída

Agios Nikólaos

Pahiá Ammos

Gaítani

Gourniá   **Π**

100

500

400

300

200

Asarí

E4

7

Vasilikí

E4

Π

←7

→8

E4

P

←7

400

300

200

7↓

10→

Episkopí

Papadianá

Ano Horió

300

300

200

300

400

500

Ierápetra

Káto Horió

O R I

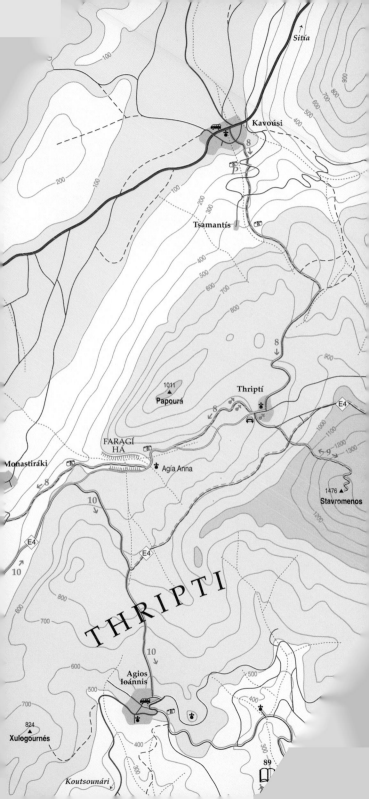

*Left and be[...]
following the [...]
of Vasiliki, the
magnificent hills
above the village
form the backdrop
for Picnic 3.*

a first glimpse of
the Libyan Sea
off to the left
as you climb
(**1h**). The track
curves right at
the top of the hill
and passes un-
der a large CAVE.
From here there
are good views
back down over
Vasiliki, the Dik-
ti range, Monas-
tiraki and the sea
off the north
coast (**1h10min**).
Follow the E4
W A Y M A R K S ,
rounding the hill
and heading in a
westerly direc-
tion. Keep left at
a fork and, very
soon, you can
see Agios Niko-
laos off to the
right, as well as
enjoying far-
reaching views
over the sea. The
track passes a
gully on the right
and, three min-
utes later, you're
off along the side
of the next hill.
As you round it
(**1h25min**), the

..scape opens out once again. A panorama of hills and
..pes in varying shades of soft greens and greys spreads
.fore you.

When the route next forks, stay left (right goes down
onto a small plain where there is a triple-forked olive tree
and some other trees). Before long (**1h50min**) the dilapidated couple of houses of **Asari** come into sight. The small
church looks intact. At a T-junction (**1h55min**) turn right
to walk to the church, passing a lovely shady place to sit,
by a large water trough. Back at the T-junction, carry
straight on along the track.

Soon, at another T-junction, turn left — leaving the E4
route off to the right (just over **2h**). Disregard a fork to the
left, and stay on the main track. The way curves to the
right and rounds a bend, giving views over the south
coast. Round the next bend, you'll also see Ierapetra, far
off to the right: your view encompasses the south and
north of the island, from the coastal flatlands around
Ierapetra on your right all the way left to Kavousi (starting
point for Walk 8) in the north. Straight ahead below you
lies Kato Horio. The track continues downhill. There are
one or two short cuts to take loops off the track but, on
the whole, the old donkey trail has been destroyed.

Staying on track, you will come within sight of Episkopi and the villages opposite it (Papadiana and Ano
Horio; **3h45min**). Eventually fork right, then take the first
left, in line with the round dome of the main village
church. Five minutes later you will be in **Episkopi**. Head
downhill until you see the main road and take the last
turn-off on the left before you reach it. This will take you
under the main road and round to the blue-domed
Byzantine church shown on page 25 and a nice quiet,
shady place. Head up the slope by the church to get to
the bus stop and the main square (**3h55min**) above it,
where you can buy a drink.

See map pages 76-77

Distance: 18km/11.2mi; 6h (allow 3h05min from Thripti to Monastiraki)

Grade: for the energetic. This walk involves a strenuous climb of lasting 2h, and surefootedness is needed for the last half hour of descent. Total ascent/descent about 700m/2300ft.

Equipment: stout shoes or boots, long trousers, sunhat, picnic, plenty of drinking water and fruit; secateurs might be useful.

How to get there: 🚌 to Kavousi (Sitia bus, Timetables 6, 8); journey time 40min

To return: 🚌 from the Monastiraki turn-off (Ierapetra bus, Timetable 5). Departs 10-15 minutes after leaving Ierapetra; journey time 35min

We have tried not to put too many 'dos' and 'don'ts' in our book; however, some walks — like this one — demand it ... if only to heighten your sheer enjoyment of it all! This is one of the walks that starts out in the east of the island, so we urge you to catch the early bus. The sunrise, particularly at the beginning and the end of summer, is simply magnificent. Also, before you embark on this walk, do take one of the nearby walks — either Walk 7 or Walk 10. From either of these you will see the splendid, dramatic cleft of the gorge at Monastiraki. At the end of this walk, you'll have the wonderful satisfaction of having walked high up behind this gorge.

This walk requires stamina, but the rewards are great, and you'll feel tremendously exhilarated — at one with the landscape — as you climb higher and higher into those splendid mountains, spellbound by the views. You can anticipate a friendly welcome in Thripti and a pleasant contrast of scenery from village to hillside — via vineyards, pasturelands and mountains, where the local people scratch a living high in the hills.

From the BUS STOP in **Kavousi**, an attractive village on the main coast road, **set off** by walking up past the CHURCH. Turn right immediately beyond it. Walk on to the VILLAGE SQUARE, at the far end of which you'll see a building with steps leading up to it. Turn left in front of it, and keep left and uphill. This route is waymarked, so keep an eye out for the daubs of paint.

Cross a track (**8min**) and, two minutes later, cross the track again — going straight over. Two minutes later, clamber back onto the track and *go left* (ignoring the waymarking to the right). If the climbing doesn't take your breath away, the views will! You can now see all the way from Agios Nikolaos to the tip of Agios Ioannis Point beyond Plaka (Picnic 8). Going left on the track, rather than following the waymarking by turning right, means you can continue for most of the walk on an old donkey trail. So walk for 40m/yds (one minute or so) and look for a footpath striking off right uphill; take this path and, within half a minute, head up right on the old cobbled donkey trail (there are old waymarks on it). Two minutes later, meet the track again and follow it to the right uphill. At a small fork, you can go right to continue on the track, but we stay left to continue on the path. You may see an old orange paint mark on the ground on the left where this section of path begins.

Now keep looking for old red waymarks; the path is very overgrown, but it *is* still there and somehow much more fulfilling to find and follow than the newer route. When you are in line with an OLD HOUSE ahead (just under **1h**), follow the path as it curves uphill to the left — don't go straight ahead across the hillside towards the house. In another 10 minutes, we will have led you up to a height of 500m/1650ft (**1h10min**). If you are inclined to suffer from vertigo, don't peer over into the gorge. Kavousi lies in an impressive spread below you now. The path comes up to a level, more open area: turn left here on a good donkey trail (**1h15min**). By this time the gradient is 1 in 3 — hard work! You will realise how aerobic walking can be as you approach the top! Ten minutes later (**1h25min**) the trail forks: keep *right and downhill,* to continue towards Thripti.

On reaching a PASS at the top of the trail (825m; **1h55min**) you will find a wide track. Turn left along it and follow it for the next half hour or so. It meanders pleasantly through an abundance of wild flowers — if it's the right time of year — and you should be able to spot some pretty pink orchids amongst them. The scenery at the top of the climb changes: it's green and hilly, with a sprinkling of vineyard terracing. Looking behind you, the large awesome mountain overlooking this landscape is Kliros. To the west of it you'll see a collection of buildings — the hamlet of Tsamantis.

More buildings soon come into sight, heralding the beginnings of Thripti. Before long, fork right, by one or two houses on the right. Three minutes later, turn left, past more old buildings. It's surprising how such seemingly unproductive land can be cultivated, and more than likely, you'll see people busily tending their vines around you, or even picking grapes — if it's early October. Look beyond the church rising up in the middle of Thripti, and you'll see the coast and sea beyond … a long way away.

Once you are in **Thripti** (**2h40min**), it's worth stopping off for a sustaining drink or two. It's a pleasant place — there is even a taverna at the eastern edge of the village that will doubtless welcome your custom if it's open — a good chance to practise some of your Greek phrases. Stay on the main track as you reach the far side of the village (where Walk 9 begins and ends). Here there is a WATER TAP, a TANK and a TROUGH over to the left, opposite the track that comes up from Kato Horio. With your back to the tap, the track from Kato Horio in front of you, and another track going off to the left (to Stavromenos), head right, going downhill on an old track, towards a few buildings, one of which has a tall cowled metal CHIMNEY. Then, half a minute along, leave the track and go left on a narrow path. This (waymarked) path curves down through vineyard terracing, round the side of a small hillock. Within a few minutes, look out for two small CONCRETE WATER HOUSES, one on either side of the path — you will know they are water houses because you can hear water flowing deep inside them.

Once past these water houses, the path reaches a track: follow it to the right. After a minute, fork right on a stony path (red waymark). Very soon you meet the same track and follow it down to the right. After a couple of bends, ignore a track coming in from the right and keep straight on, as indicated by a red arrow (20 minutes from Thripti; **3h15min**).

In five minutes, go right, still on the track and, very soon, at a fork, go right again (the left-hand fork goes to a taverna). Stay on this track; it's pleasant to wander through these pine trees without having to watch every step. Some 40 minutes from Thripti (**3h35min**) you meet another track (the surface is greyish in colour): follow it to the right downhill; almost at once, it's sandy again. Very shortly you *could* take a small waymarked path off to the right, but it's much easier to stay on the track.

Fifty minutes from Thripti (**3h45min**), you will have a tremendous view straight through the top of the gorge and over to the village of Vasiliki (Walk 7). Three minutes later, pass the small church of Agia Anna on your left and, just beyond it, as the track curves to the right, take the right-hand fork — it follows the old footpath route. Two to three minutes further on, a lesser track goes off to the right. Keep straight on here. Rounding the top of **Ha Gorge** (1h15min from Thripti; **4h10min**), you'll enjoy a fabulous view over Pahia Ammos and the bay. Here keep on the lower track and, five minutes later, you will reach the lowest point in the track, where there is a river bed and some oleanders. Cross the river bed and then climb the steeply-rising ground ahead, where a narrow path curves to the right. Follow this footpath as it gently ascends; it is a bit overgrown so, as a guide, use the grey stones beside it. The path soon curves round to the left and then to the right, to a view over the north coast.

Ha Gorge, from the track above Monastiraki

Soon (1h35min from Thripti; **4h30min**) you can feast your eyes on another fantastic panorama. You're now high above the main road, with views of Ierapetra, the setting for Walk 10, and all the way round north to Agios Nikolaos. Looking out from this marvellous viewing point, you also have a perfect lookout over Vasiliki and the hills of Walk 7, shown in the photographs on pages 78 and 79. Beyond them, to the west, lie the hills of Lasithi (Walks 15, 16 and 18). On more than one occasion, we have stood here transfixed, marvelling at the changing colours, patterns and textures of this wonderful landscape. The path *is* there; pick your way amongst all the fallen trees (the remains of a devastating fire in 1987) and look out for waymarks helping you to find your way. You are heading south now.

Two hours from Thripti (**4h55min**), the path divides: go right at a red arrow waymark, making sure you don't go on to Kato Horio. About three minutes later, look out for a patch of rockface facing west (on your left) and a small landslide coming down from it. There are waymarks either side of the path. Head downhill, initially on the landslide of stones and rocks, then search for a small path heading off to the right — due north, towards the coast. This narrow path winds its way down the hillside to Monastiraki. After 20-25 minutes on this path, you reach a track (2h25min from Thripti; **5h20min**). Follow this track to the right, passing above the top part of **Monastiraki**, enjoying the view shown on page 83. After 10 minutes, another track comes in from the left, but carry on to the right, curving downhill and then round to the left. In another 10 minutes turn left on a track, then fork right. Fork right again and, at the next fork, go left.

Some 2h55min from Thripti (**5h 50min**), you meet the main track into Monastiraki: turn left here. Ten minutes later you arrive at the main road. The BUS STOP is on the left (3h05min from Thripti; **6h**).

9 THRIPTI TO STAVROMENOS AND RETURN

See map pages 76-77 **Distance:** 10km/6.2mi; 3h10min
Grade: a long, steep climb and descent of 700m/2300ft
Equipment: stout shoes or boots, sunhat, picnic, plenty of drinking water and fruit, long trousers
How to get there and return: 🚗 only accessible by car to Thripti (via Kato Horio; 4-wheel drive recommended — see page 20). Leave your car in the open parking area near the water tank and tap.

Getting to Thripti is a challenge in itself, but this particular leg-stretch takes you from there up above the clouds — to a small mountaintop church. From the top you can see far out over the south and north coasts of the island and really feel a sense of achievement.

Facing the TAP and WATER TANK in **Thripti**, **start out** by taking the track to the right of them. (This track curls up to the highest house in the village; the track straight ahead is where Walk 8 comes into Thripti.) When you are about in line with the church, turn sharp right uphill on a steep path (**5min**). Within 15-20 paces you will see WAYMARKING on a wall on the left. Pass a WAYMARKED RUINED BUILDING on the left and follow waymarks up through more tumble-down buildings. You will be climbing up through vineyard terraces by now. The very narrow path could well have water running down it in places, as it's the irrigation system for the terraces of fruit trees and vines. You need to keep in line with the church in Thripti and continue up via more tumbledown buildings, some of which bear old

At the chapel of Afendis Christos atop Stavromenos

Inside Afendis Christos

waymarks. The path bends left around and above terraces. Here's where long trousers come in useful, as the path becomes very overgrown. You are well above the village of Thripti by now and, as you walk along the terracing, look up to the right, to another old building, for more waymarks.

The path comes up onto the TRACK again (**30min**), which you follow to the left. There are buildings up on your right. The track curves slightly, round to the right. There's an ARROW WAYMARK on your right, and the continuation of your path veers sharply back to the right, climbing up off the track (it was faintly waymarked when we were last here). Go up left in front of a building and then bend right on the path, round the back of the buildings. The path splits at the corner of the building; go right. Keep left at the next house and go round the back of it. The path bends round and up to a track above the house. Turn left on this very rough rubble track. When the track divides (**45min**), look for a WAYMARK ARROW pointing up right into pine trees. Very soon, at the next fork, go left; the path is waymarked now.

The path moves out of the pines and meets a wide track. Beyond this point there was a wonderful path which climbed incredibly steeply up Stavromenos. You *may* still be able to find it, but bulldozers have chucked rubble onto it, making it difficult to find from here. Waymarking firmly directs you onto the *track,* which you follow for just under an hour to the SUMMIT of **Stavromenos** (**1h40min**).

Having enjoyed the peace of the small windswept chapel of **Afendis Christos** and the dramatic view over the north and south coasts — and doubtless picnicked — turn round and head back to **Thripti** (**3h10min**) for some *real* sustenance — like *raki.*

?starts on pages 76-77 and ends on page 89

?ance: 21.5km/13.3mi; 6h40min

?rade: moderate-strenuous; a long walk with a gradual ascent of about ?00m/2000ft at the start and a descent of 500m/1600ft from Agios Ioannis; all on tracks. Note that there is virtually no shade on the ascent.

Equipment: stout shoes, sunhat, picnic, water, long trousers, swimwear

How to get there: 🚐 to Episkopi (Ierapetra bus; Timetable 5); journey time 40min

To return: 🚐 from Agia Fotia to Ierapetra (Timetables 10, 22). Bus from Sitia departs Agia Fotia about 1h after leaving Sitia; bus from Makrigialos departs Agia Fotia 5 minutes after leaving Makrigialos; journey time 25min. Change to 🚐 from Ierapetra to Agios Nikolaos/Iraklion: departures almost hourly (Timetable 5); journey time 1h

Short walks

1 **Episkopi to Agios Ioannis** (11.5km/7.2mi; 4h10min). Grade (ascent), equipment and access as main walk. Return on 🚐 from Agios Ioannis to Agia Fotia (not in the timetables: departs 13.00 *Wednesdays only*; then bus from Agia Fotia as above). Or telephone from the *cafeneion* in Agios Ioannis for a taxi from Agia Fotia or Ierapetra. Follow the main walk to Agios Ioannis.

2 **Agios Ioannis to Agia Fotia** (10km/6.2mi; 2h30min). Fairly easy descent of 500m/1600ft. Equipment as above. 🚐 to Ierapetra (Timetable 5), then 🚐 to Agios Ioannis (not in the timetables: departs 12.15 *Wednesdays only*; journey time 45min). Return as main walk. Use the notes on page 89, starting at the 4h10min-point.

Here's a walk that leads you gently up and over the Thripti Mountains and to the south coast, where the landscape is very different from the north. Since it follows tracks all the way, there is no need to watch your footing;

Climbing into the hills above the village of Episkopi on the Thripti track

As we leave Ag Ioannis, a churc looks as if it has b built of crazy pavin with silver-grey domes, comes into view.

you can stride out, enjoying the scenery. To finish, how about a swim in the Libyan Sea?

The bus stops not far past the road sign for **Episkopi**, just beyond the large village church. **Start out** by walking back north along the bus route, until you reach the 'EPISKOPI' SIGN at the Agios Nikolaos end of the village. Here take the track down to the right (just by the sign showing the end of the 25km/h speed limit). After a minute you'll pass a small CHURCH. Join the bypass road, cross it with care and turn left. After a few metres/yards turn right into an asphalt side-road signposted to Kato Horio and Papadiana. Walk a few metres up this road; then, just past a water distribution point, turn left on a track. The track passes to the right of a WINDMILL, where it forks into three. Keep to the centre track. Stay on this track until you come to a fork (**15min**): go right here and, one minute later, fork right again.

You're now climbing a little, with quite gentle hillside contours creating the landscape ahead. At the next T-junction (**20min**), turn left. Pass a CHURCH on your left (**35min**), beyond which the track curves round to the right (the photograph on pages 86-87 was taken here). A minute past the church there is a good picnicking spot, with glorious views all round. Then the north coast comes into sight (**45min**). After passing a covered WATER TROUGH and WELL HEAD on your right (**50min**; listen out for the sound of rushing water), keep on this main track, which almost doubles back on the way you came. Now you'll have a slightly steeper climb as you really get into the hills. You can still see across the island from north to south. The town nestling over to your right is Vasiliki, where we start Walk 7. You are now on the main Thripti track, which is also part of the E4 route.

When you reach a fork (**57min**) with a signpost in Greek pointing the way to Thripti (ΘΡΙΠΤΗ) or right to elima (ΣΕΛΙΜΑ; a mountain), continue towards Thripti. most an hour later you come to another fork (**1h48min**), another signpost in Greek: Thripti is straight ahead,

Anna (a church below Thripti) is to the left. Keep
on the E4 here, continuing uphill amidst even more
endid views.

The next signpost (**2h30min**) points to Thripti straight
on or Agios Ioannis to the right: turn right uphill here for
Agios Ioannis. (Agios Ioannis is also written in Greek, with
an arrow, both in red paint, on a rock at the beginning of
this track.) The track weaves its way around the mountain
and through pine woods. When you come to a Y-fork
(**2h40min**) head left, as indicated by a red arrow on a rock.
At the next fork (**3h07min**), turn left and descend a track
covered with loose stones — watch your footing. At the
next fork (**3h30min**) again keep left downhill. Three
minutes later, ignore a track joining you from the left;
keep straight downhill.

At last Agios Ioannis comes into view (**3h40min**), and
you reach another fork. Either branch will take you to
Agios Ioannis (and don't worry when the village disappears from view for a short time). When you emerge in
the small square at **Agios Ioannis** (**4h10min**), you will find
a welcome *cafeneion* (from where you can telephone for
a taxi, should you decide to call it a day here). After some
refreshment, explore village with its attractive church.

To make for Agia Fotia, leave Agios Ioannis on the

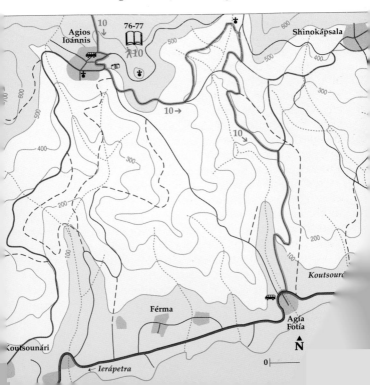

KOUTSOUNARI ROAD. After a few bends the road c.
round to the right, and the church shown on page
comes into view down on your right. But we walk aw
from the church, taking a left turn onto another track. N
far along, we round the fertile valley leading from Agios
Ioannis to the sea. On the descent you will enjoy some
good views back up to Agios Ioannis just behind you. As
the main village disappears from sight (**4h25min**), stay on
the right-hand, lower track. Then, five minutes later, take
the higher, left-hand track (the two tracks run almost
parallel here; keep to the higher one).

As you round a bend, the scene changes from one of
green cultivation to open landscape. An enormous mountain spreads before you, with a tiny church as a centre-
piece. It is useful to *keep this church in mind* as a land-
mark, as there are many new tracks criss-crossing the
way, going to various olive groves and smallholdings.
After about 10 minutes (from turning the bend), you'll see
another track going up to the left — ignore it, and stay on
the main route here. After another five minutes, ignore
another track going off left and keep on the main track.
In another five minutes, stay on the main (lower) track to
the right. Immediately after crossing a small stream, this
track forks. The right-hand fork is your ongoing route, but
first take the left-hand fork to make a short detour to a
pleasant resting spot, next to a church surrounded by tall
cool pines and olive groves, beside a gushing stream.
Then retrace your steps from this cul-de-sac and take the
other fork. It leads across an olive grove and another
stream set in a gully. After crossing the stream, the path
bends left up an incline (facing the hills). When you reach
a track, turn right and follow it for 20 minutes, then fork
right. The track curves round from the sea (**5h40min**) and
meets an asphalt road two minutes later: turn right. Two
or three minutes further on, at a three-way fork, keep right.

About half an hour later (**6h15min**), you will see plastic
greenhouses down in the valley to the left. Now there is
only 25 minutes between you and the lovely sparkling
sea at Agia Fotia. What about a hang glider? The track
now turns away from the sea and back towards the mountains, giving you a chance to look out over the hills you've
just crossed. Curve round the greenhouses and soon
come to the MAIN SOUTH COAST ROAD. Turn right and, a bit
 urther on, you'll see the sign for **Agia Fotia** beach. Just
  yond it is the BUS STOP (**6h40min**). Remember to stand
    he inland side of the road for your journey to Ierapetra.

See also photograph pages 16-17

Distance: 11km/7mi; 3h30min

Grade: easy to moderate, with a gradual (long) ascent of 530m/1740ft and a descent of 430m/1400ft; possibility of vertigo

Equipment: stout shoes, sunhat, water (none en route), picnic

How to get there: 🚌 to Sfaka (Sitia bus, Timetables 6, 8); journey time 1 hour. Or 🚗 to Sfaka and return on the same bus to your car.

To return: 🚌 from Tourloti (Sitia bus, Timetables 6, 8). Departs Tourloti 30min after leaving Sitia; journey time to Agios Nikolaos 1h05min.

Here's a pleasant loop that leads you through hillside pastureland and the heart of a farming community. Open countryside fringes the mountains, and you're never far from the sight of the sea.

As you approach the village of **Sfaka**, the bus stops by a KIOSK on the right, where a side road leads off uphill. **Start out** by walking back west towards Agios Nikolaos on the main road. Soon you'll see long shallow steps leading up off the road, with railings alongside them. Climb these and, at the top, turn right onto a concrete road which heads through the village houses up towards the mountain behind them. Soon the concrete road changes into an earthen track (**5min**). Three minutes later, ignore a track sprouting off to the left. Start curving round to the right on the main track, then take the donkey path that goes off to the left. Soon you'll have a nice view back over Sfaka and its church. The path changes from cobbles to a rough finish just before rejoining the main track (**12min**). Here you can look out straight over Sfaka all the way to Tourloti, your destination — your way is over the mountains ahead. Set just off the road, a little way beyond Tourloti, you'll see Mirsini — the next coastal village on the road to Sitia.

As you rejoin the track at this good lookout point, don't be misled by the inviting-looking track opposite. It doesn't lead to the perfect picnic spot — unless you want to sit in someone's garden. Turn left and, after a couple of bends in the route, you'll be looking straight across to Askordalia (1238m/ 4060ft), the highest peak in

Tourloti

the Orno range. The coastline is fast receding, but the ascent is quite gradual. The track crosses a dried-up stream which the local people are now using as a RUBBISH TIP (**18min**). Curve around and, within a minute, just where you can see the main road below you, strike off left up another small donkey path that may well be somewhat overgrown. As it forms a 'T', go left; then walk on and head towards the stone wall up above. The path turns into rubble and widens out. You can see the bends of the main track below you — proving that you're shortening your walk. When the path rejoins the track (**30min**), there is a building to your right, at the edge of the terracing. Turn left here. You can see Lastros now with its church in the foreground.

The track cuts through vineyard terracing (**35min**); there's the odd fig tree here, too. When the track splits (**50min**), keep to the upper track (right) and go on round the bend. From here it's easy to make out the half-hidden Psira ('Flea') Island and the small dot of an island called Agios Nikolaos, both just off the coast at Mohlos. When the track divides again (**1h**), again keep to the upper level (left).

ʋu see the new church again, which you first saw as
climbed up through the village at the start of the walk.
ɔn pass some DWELLINGS and ANIMAL SHELTERS off to the
ft, but don't take the track down to them. You've been
able to enjoy level walking for some time now, but soon
the way starts to climb again (gradually), after you pass
by a WINNOWING AND THRESHING CIRCLE on your right
(**1h05min**). You are just behind the CHURCH; it is between
you and Sfaka. When the track forks (**1h10min**), keep
right, to the upper way. Then stay on this track as it bends
round.

Ten minutes later, come to a T-junction with a tree at
the corner. Turn right and head towards the mountains.
Soon you'll pass deep STONE WELLS (similar in construction
to Minoan wells) and go through DOUBLE METAL GATES
(**1h25min**). Five minutes later, rounding a deep curve to
the left, you'll have a good view of a gorge below to the
right, as it heads down to the sea. Then you'll lose sight
of the sea altogether. Soon spot another collection of
stone buildings up to the right.

A church comes into sight (**1h40min**). A few minutes
later, you pass through another pair of METAL GATES. Then
the track divides again. Take the left-hand fork, leading
towards the church. Before long, having passed the
CHURCH, you'll approach a group of dwellings on a stony
outcrop. This is **Platanos** (**1h45min**), the heart of the
farming and shepherd community enlivening this landscape. Their livelihood is spread out all around you —
fruit trees, almond and walnut trees, vines, figs and
pastureland. Massive, rounded mountains encircle you.
As you walk towards a STONE WALL AND A SHELTER, the track
bends round to the right. Follow it round, then bend left
again.

Soon (**1h50min**) the track abuts a line of scree. Just
before here, turn left on the track that heads towards some
buildings. You'll be walking seawards again, although the
sea is not yet in sight. Five minutes past the turn-off, the
track becomes a path and leads down through a small
vineyard, to a GATE. Go through the gate — there's a HOUSE
on your left. Look for a trail going off up the hill ahead of
you and make for it. There may be some fences here; if
so, look for a way through, or you may have to climb over
them. This cobbled trail runs high above the bed of a
dried-up river, which years ago would have coursed this
way to the sea.

Suddenly, through a V in the mountains ahead, yɔ

see the coast and the glistening blue sea (**2h**). The 'dinosaur's back' of rock on the far side of the tree-lined river bed arches towards the sea now, just as the trail gives way to a path. This path turns away from the river bed, to the right. Some people may find this path a bit unnerving, especially if they are prone to vertigo, because it is so high. However, the drops are not sheer, and the walking is easy and level.

Buildings come into sight up ahead on the left, at the end of the path and, if you look towards the sea, you'll see the granite quarry scar above Mohlos again and little Psira Island, still slightly hidden behind the coast. Once you reach here, away from the edge of the river bed gorge, the possibility of vertigo is lessened. And then you're back on a track again (**2h20min**; there's more wire netting just before the path meets the track). Join the track and turn left, towards the buildings. In ten minutes, this track passes between a stone wall and a fence. From here there are lovely views of your destination, Tourloti, the north coast, Sfaka to your left, and Mirsini to the right. This is a nice place to take a break before descending for the last part of the walk.

As the track begins to descend now and makes its first loop, you'll see a path going off straight ahead. Follow it until it joins the track again. Continue down to the right on the track until, at the next bend, you can again use the path as a short cut. When the path splits, take the lower fork, to the right. When you next meet the track, step down over rocks, walk right, round the next bend and take a path off to the right. Watch your footing — the stones are loose. Join the track again and pass to the right of vineyard terracing. Soon (**2h50min**) you'll be taking

Left: in the Orno range, high above Sfaka. Right: near the end of the walk, the path skirts an olive grove interlaced with thick clumps of thyme.

another short-cut path. This one is angled back from the track. It starts out just beyond a slab-like piece of flat rock. The path becomes overgrown and goes through knee-high undergrowth. It skirts round vine-growing plots and passes behind a stone building. The path widens out beyond the building. Look for the path going left, towards Tourloti. Continue on it, and soon you will meet the track again. Turn left and continue on down; within yards, at a cross-track, turn right. Then, as a track forks back to the left, continue on for a few yards and take the path going off left. This path gets wider as we near the outskirts of Tourloti. Rejoining the track, turn left, then take the path off right again. Then join the track once more and follow it to the right downhill. You'll pass a STONE BUILDING WITH A COWLED METAL CHIMNEY, as the track bends left. A minute or so past here, take the secondary track curving back off to the right. Within a very short distance, it appears to end. Walk down to the right, onto a path (there's a wall on the right of this path). Curve round a DERELICT BUILDING on the left. Meet the main track again (**3h15min**) and turn right; there's a large fig tree on your left. After about 200m/yds, go left, down off the track and onto a path that skirts olive trees and then descends beneath another fig tree.

As you meet the track again, turn left and you'll be level with Tourloti. Walk on towards the village and find the main road just ahead below you. A blue and white sign points you towards **Tourloti** (**3h30min**). As the bus goes into the village from the main road, why not aim for the centre right now and have a well-earned rest and refreshing drink, before going to the bus shelter?

Distance: 7.5km/4.7mi; 2h20min

Grade: straightforward gorge walking, path overgrown in parts. Overall descent 350m/1150ft

Equipment: stout shoes, sunhat, water, picnic, long trousers, swimwear

How to get there: 🚌 to Sitia (Timetables 6, 8); journey time 1h45min. Change to 🚐 to Zakros (Timetable 11); journey time 1h10min. Or 🚗 to Zakros and bus from Kato Zakros back to your car.

To return: 🚌 from Kato Zakros to Sitia (Timetable 11), then 🚌 to Agios Nikolaos (Timetables 6, 8); journey times as above.

Alternative walk: Valley of the Dead (3.5km/2.2mi; 1h). Start at the top of the gorge itself, rather than in Zakros. Access and return as main walk, but stay on the bus beyond Zakros and alight at the sign to the 'GORGE' (on the right-hand side of the road, just before a major bend to the right and under telephone wires). By 🚗, park in Kato Zakros and take a bus to the starting point, or park at the head of the gorge (where there is a walking map) and take the bus back to your car. Descend the track on the north side of the road, immediately opposite the sign. When the track turns left in a few minutes, continue straight on. A steep, step-like section involves negotiation by backside, before you meet the main gorge 10 minutes downhill. Turn right.

This walk through the Valley of the Dead (Faragi Nekron) is one of our favourites. You can either start in the village of Zakros or from the top of the gorge (Alternative walk). Starting from Zakros, you get the benefit of a pretty village and some lush gardens, vines, vegetables, olives and flowers. Not only is the walk splendid, but the goal, Kato Zakros, is a real haven (once the lunchtime coach parties have moved on), with the bonus of a Minoan site. Plan to stay the night if there's room.

Start out in the village square in **Zakros**: look towards the two crosses of the main church visible from here. Walk towards this church, past houses. As you draw level with the church, fork right and follow the village street as it leads downhill. Continue by crossing a water channel. Just ahead, there's a bridge with a glorious splash of bougainvillea on its left side, and sploshing water invites a bottle refill — even though you are just at the start of the walk!

When you come to crossroads, turn right and walk on past the houses, leaving the village on a concrete track (**10min**). You pass a small concrete-block storage building on the right. Just beyond it, take the narrow WAYMARKED PATH that leads off left through olive

96

ees and via animal enclosures. The path *is* waymarked,
but the first waymark (on a low stone wall on the left) is
likely to be hidden by undergrowth. Reaching a watercourse, go straight over and turn right on the far side. Stay
by the watercourse for about 200m/yds, after which the
path enters an open area. Look left: there's a stone wall
with waymarking on it. The route bends up and around
to the left, becoming concreted as it rises steeply (a
waymarked chicken coop is at the point where it starts to
rise). Once up the far side, bend round to the right (more
waymarks) and head towards olive trees. Ignore a break
in the wall and a path going off to the right. The path you
are on is now running beside a WATER CHANNEL. Fork right,
heading south (**20min**), looking carefully for waymarks.
(The watercourse may be running down onto the turning.)
Keep heading south, on a level contour, heading towards
a MESH GATE. Go through this first gate, making sure you
close it behind you if that was how you found it, and walk
down towards a CONCRETE BUILDING. From here you can
easily see the path that heads right towards the gorge. Go
through another GATE (**25min**) and look up very slightly to
find the path continuing. The watercourse running down
on the right is an attractive plane tree-lined ribbon going
south with you.

By this time (**30min**) you really feel you're in gorge
country and, very soon, you will be down by a channel
of rushing water. The path runs under some oleander and
moves away from the water. As the path meets a NETTING

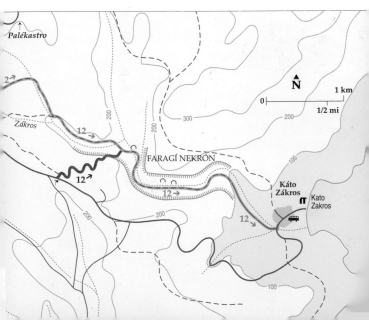

Left: tranquil Kato Zakros, after the crowds have gone. Below: in the gorge. Some of the caves you'll see on your descent are Minoan burial chambers, which have given the gorge its name, 'Valley of the Dead' (Faragi Nekron).

FENCE, head right. It's then necessary to climb over the fence to follow the waymarking; a narrow path leads alongside an irrigation channel (**35min**).

At one point (**40min**) cross over the water channel and turn sharp right, to pick up the path which now runs to the left of the water. Before long the waymarking leads across a dry river bed, then points you to the left. Walk over the half-covered water channel. When the path comes to a 'T' on the far side, keep right. Follow the way-marking, going back over the irrigation channel and back down into the river bed. Watch for the waymarks.

A little over 3km along (**55min**) the landscape opens out in front of you and the lower (main) part of the gorge is ahead. The rest of the walk is fairly straightforward. The path soon becomes a track and, at the end of the lower gorge, you turn left on another wide sweep of purply-pink track — the colour is characteristic of the region. You pass a banana plantation on the right (**1h25min**) and vines and pomegranates on the left. Soon you can see Kato Zakros ahead. Continue along the easy track, to the welcoming sea and few houses of **Kato Zakros** (**2h20min**).

PEFKI GORGE

Distance: 16km/10mi; 5h15min

Grade: moderate ascents and descents of about 450m/1475ft overall; some agility required

Equipment: stout shoes or boots, sunhat, picnic, water

How to get there and return: 🚌 to Ierapetra (Timetable 5); journey time 1h. Change to bus along south coast to Makrigialos (Ierapetra/Sitia bus, Timetable 10, or Ierapetra/Makrigialos bus, Timetable 22); journey time 30min. Use the same buses to return. Or 🚗 to/from Makrigialos.

This is a lovely circular walk — a good day's outing — from Makrigialos, a low-key seaside place (Picnic 6) just east of Koutsouras on the south coast. It's usually possible to find a room to rent here, should you want to stay overnight. The Pefki Gorge was used by the villagers to take produce down to the coast, and the walk runs along the top edge of the gorge before descending into it. As you descend, you will see the houses of Aspro Potamos (White River), which the villagers originally built as overnight accommodation.

Start out on the main south coast road at **Makrigialos**: take the concrete road inland, signposted 'AG STEPHANOS 7KM'. Walk uphill; the concrete surface becomes asphalt at the outskirts of the village. You are heading towards a small church up on the hillside to the right. Climbing inland, you start to have a nice view of the coast below (**15min**), over Makrigialos. Just past the church, which is set back from the road, take the first track going left (**19min**); it winds behind the CHURCH. When you come to a fork (**35min**), keep right uphill. Later, on reaching a staggered T-junction in the track, go to the left (if you first walk a short way to the right, you will see that you're on the bend of the asphalt road). After walking to the left, you come to another Y-fork: go right, heading uphill again. This track gets rocky and stony and within a few minutes becomes a path which must have been an old donkey trail.

The path takes you onto the asphalt road. Look left, diagonally, for a path continuing steeply up the far side of the road. Very shortly (within about three minutes) the path meets the road again. Cross straight over, now on a wide trail. This path is cutting loops off the road. When you meet the road again, turn left and, within half a minute (on a bend just before a huge bluff), continue on the narrow walled-in donkey trail leading off to the right.

You snatch a last glimpse of Makrigialos behind you in the V of the cliff (**1h15min**). This stretch has a nice view over a small fertile valley down to the right. Five minutes

later, you catch sight of the church on the pinnacle abo▸
Pefki in the middle of the valley ahead.

Ten minutes later (**1h30min**) pass the sign for **Agio**.
Stefanos and the beginning of the village. In the middle
of the village, next to the CHURCH, follow the sign pointing
right to 'PEFKI'. The asphalted road now becomes concrete
and, on the outskirts of the village the way becomes rough
track. As you approach a CHURCH on the far side of Agios
Stefanos, ignore a fork off left to this church; follow the
track round to the right. Very soon after rounding the
church, having come round a bluff of rock, look up to the
left: you will see Pefki church rising in the distance.
Round the next bend, the beginnings of the village itself
come into sight. Notice, about 100m/yds before you
come into the edge of Pefki, a map of the gorge and a path
leading off to the right; this is your return route. Walk on
into the centre of **Pefki** (**2h30min**).

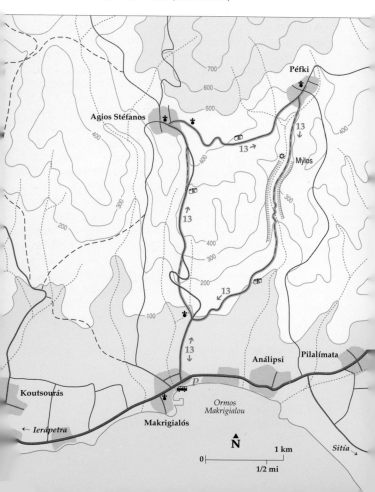

When you are ready to return to the coast, having explored, or had something to eat, or both, head back out of Pefki the way you came in. Three minutes outside the village, look for the path passed earlier; it is clearly signposted 'GORGE' and goes down to the left about 100m/yds beyond the edge of the village. As you leave the road, keep left and you will see a waymarked donkey trail going down the hill. This is the old mule track down to the coast. About 500m/yds from the top it meets a dirt track. Turn right on the track for a few paces, then pick up the continuation of your path, going left downhill through the olive groves. Cross over a small WATERCOURSE, which will be dry in summer (15min from Pefki; **2h45min**). You're descending beside fragrant pines. As the donkey trail comes down into a more open area, you come upon a shady picnic spot with a WOODEN BENCH AND TABLE on the left and a sign pointing right to the gorge (30min from Pefki; **3h**). The gorge walls are visible from here. A little further downhill you pass **Mylos**, an old mill in an open area, just by another MAP. In spring there is the sound of water far down to the left. Just over half an hour from Pefki (**3h05min**), at a fork where arrows point down towards the gorge, you see the beginning of the gorge walls. In spring there is a small waterfall here.

Fifty minutes from Pefki (**3h20min**) a SIGNPOST points down left to the gorge and straight on to Pisokamino. (There is another map and waterfall here.) Head left, down towards the gorge. The lovely WATERFALL is just visible on your right, cascading in two tiers. This narrow path descends steeply into the gorge. Walking carefully down the path brings you to water level. Cross over the stream and pick up the path on the far side — catching a glimpse of the houses of Aspro Potamos. The path goes down into the stream bed, where there are waterfalls in spring. It *looks* as if you have to jump down one of them (it's only just under a metre/3ft high, but it feels a bit higher if you're clambering down it!). But, if you search about, you *don't* have to jump down: keep to the left and you can push your way through and then over the water-course.

But agility *is* soon required, as there is a steep boulder to get down. Beyond that, after picking your way through the rocks for a few moments, you come to some railings on the right and, from here on, the route is easier. You then come to 18 metal steps which take you down a sheer drop in the river bed. (You might notice a lot of fire devastation amongst the pine trees around here.) A second set of 20 metal steps helps you negotiate another steep drop. Beyond these steps, you cross the watercourse again.

Eventually emerging from the gorge on a rough track (1h40min from Pefki; **4h10min**), you come upon another MAP. Walk right (to the left is the route to Agiorgio Samakines and the rough road up to Pefki from the Sunwing Hotel on the coast). The track bends down to the watercourse in one big loop over stepping stones and, just over two hours from Pefki (**4h35min**), the whole coast is spread out before you. Keep straight on, ignoring a track going down to the left. When you come to a T-junction, turn left, down towards the coast. Five minutes later the rough track meets the asphalt road you followed on your ascent to Pefki: turn left downhill and follow it back to the MAIN SOUTH COAST ROAD at **Makrigialos** (2h45min from Pefki; **5h15min**).

In the gorge (about three and a half hours into the walk)

LIMNES • VRISES • LIMNES

Distance: 4km/2.5mi; 1h30min
Grade: easy, with an overall ascent of 100m/330ft on the outward leg
Equipment: comfortable shoes, sunhat, water
How to get there and return: 🚌 towards Iraklion (Timetables 1, 8, 14);
ask to be put off for Limnes (journey time about 15min). The bus stops
only on the national highway (where you will also pick it up on your
return). If you're travelling from Agios Nikolaos, walk ahead (west) along
the highway for a few minutes and follow the signposts and main tarmac
road into Limnes. If coming from Iraklion, walk back along the highway
in the direction you have come and take the first left and then the first
right, to follow the tarmac road into Limnes. Once in Limnes, follow the
road around past a *cafeneion* with plenty of chairs under a pergola on
your right, then past a shrine and a round stone and slate well. There is
now a small bridge on your left, where the walk starts. Or 🚗: entering
Limnes from the eastern (Agios Nikolaos) end, drive through the village
towards Neapolis and park near a stone wind pump, just before a small
bridge on the left, where the walk starts.

This is a very pleasant, straightforward walk via Houmeriakos, affording a good look at three villages with
winding streets and lots of character, and a great view
from the top of the climb, at Vrises.

Start the walk in **Limnes** by crossing the SMALL BRIDGE
on the left. There is a blue SIGNPOST for an olive oil factory
on the corner (in Greek). As you cross the bridge, you can
see the villages of Houmeriakos and Vrises up in the hills
in front of you. The path passes through fields and vege-
table patches, with many stone and metal wind pumps,
citrus, almond and olive trees, and vines. Before long the
route comes to a junction where there is a taverna straight
ahead (it's a big one, used for village weddings, baptisms
and celebrations). Turn left, and then go right immediately, onto a good concrete surface.

Reach another junction (**5min**), again with many water
pumps, and carry on straight across. The road is flanked
by two low stone walls. Two minutes later pass a small
CHURCH on the right and then, about 10 minutes later,
walk into **Houmeriakos (15min)**. The large village CHURCH
is on the left. Go on uphill and turn right, passing a large
SHRINE on the right. Next comes the village 'square', with
a TELEPHONE BOX; turn sharp left, up the hill, here. Keep
right at the CHURCH WITH AN ARCHED PORTICO and then pass
a fresh spring-water FOUNTAIN (**17min**). Now following a
broken concrete track uphill, ignore paths coming in from
either side. At a T-JUNCTION (with a high stone wall ahead),
turn right and then left uphill, passing a BRICKED-UP ARCH-
WAY on the left. Continue to wind your way up through
the village. Ten minutes from entering Houmeriakos you
have a good view back to Limnes.

Houmeriakos

Carry on left uphill and then curve to the right. Soon (**25min**) you have left Houmeriakos behind and you are walking through open countryside on a concrete track, heading for a church you can see up on the right. Ignore tracks coming in from either side and carry on uphill. When you reach the CHURCH (**30min**), turn left on a rough, sandy track. Keep left as Vrises comes into sight. The track becomes concreted. When it makes the first sharp bend to the left, strike off right and then, almost immediately, take the somewhat overgrown path to the left. (Continuing on track would, however, take you to the same place.) The path ends at the outskirts of **Vrises**, by a SHRINE. Walk round to the left and up shallow steps. At the intersection go straight across and continue up stone steps. As you wend your way uphill, look up a side street to see house number 94 and turn right up this street to continue uphill. Turn right at the top, on the MAIN NEAPOLIS/LASITHI ROAD. There are one or two *cafeneions* along this road (**45min**).

Return the same way to **Limnes** (**1h30min**).

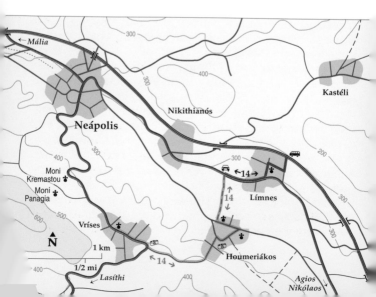

MESA LASITHI • TAPES • KRITSA

p ends on pages 56-57 **Distance:** 19km/12mi; 6h

Grade: moderate, with a gradual ascent of 350m/1150ft and a descent of 850m/2800ft. Some loose scree is crossed; danger of vertigo.

Equipment: stout shoes or boots, sunhat, water, picnic, long trousers

How to get there: 🚌 to Malia (Timetable 1); journey time 30min. Change to 🚌 to Lasithi (Timetable 25); journey time 1h30min. (Check in advance whether the bus is going to Mesa Lasithi; if not, take the bus to Tzermiado and a taxi from there to Mesa Lasithi.)

To return: 🚌 from Kritsa to Agios Nikolaos (Timetable 3); journey time 15min.

Short walk: Tapes to Kritsa (6km/3.75mi; 1h50min). Fairly easy. Equipment as above. 🚌 to Tapes (not in the timetables): departs Agios Nikolaos 06.30, 14.00 daily *(check!);* journey time 35min. Pick up the main walk at the 4h10min-point and follow it to the end (map pages 56-57).

Alternative walk: Mesa Lasithi to Tapes (13km/8mi; 4h). Grade and access as main walk; return by 🚌 from Tapes (not in the timetables): departs 14.45 daily *(do check!);* journey time 30min. Follow the main walk to Tapes.

A vivid picture will remain in your mind when you've completed this walk: the dramatic beauty and moods of the mountains to the north, overlooking the wild, steep valley of Potami. *Do* try to tackle the *entire* walk — even if you do it in two parts (the Short and Alternative walks). Since the walk starts out at 885m/2900ft, not much climbing is involved. You'll cover a good distance without getting too tired.

From the bus, look out for the road sign for Mesa Lasithi as you dip down into the Lasithi Plateau. Once off the bus in **Mesa Lasithi**, **start out** by walking back the way you came on the bus, following the road through the village of **Nikiforidon**. The leave the main road on a hairpin bend (**15min**): take the donkey trail to the left of a small grassy track that heads off to the right here. (It is waymarked with an orange and black '01' IN A DIAMOND.) There are good views of the Lasithi Plateau from this trail, but do watch your footing as well, since the stones are quite loose. Don't expect to see the famous windmills from here; you'll get a better look at windmills from Tzermiado (Walk 18) or Psychro (Walk 16). When you meet a WAY-MARKED track (**23min**), turn right. Now there are excellent views of the Lasithi Plateau (Picnic 9). Soon (**32min**) the track becomes a stony trail that heads uphill (WAYMARKED).

Just before you reach the (cross-less) church of **Agios Apostoli**, take the grassy trail heading left (**37min**; WAY-MARKED). If it's the right time of the year, you'll have a blaze of scarlet poppies either side of you. After two minutes the trail narrows considerably, and the landscape to the left is very grey-green, tones that stay with you throughout the walk. On coming to a track (just over **45min**), tu left. When the track bends round to the right, keep straig ahead on the stonier route. Within a minute, pass a for back off to the right. After half a minute, your way divides. Take the right-hand, higher track and keep straight on uphill. You will see a HUT down to the left, surrounded by rock-strewn hills and the occasional almond tree. When you meet another track (**1h05min**) fork left, straight uphill.

Pass another small stone CHURCH up to your right (**1h22min**). Keep left just beyond it, passing a stone WATER TROUGH. Shortly after that, stay on the track, heading right. Soon (**1h30min**) there are magnificent sweeping views to the left. You will be looking over the route the bus took into Mesa Lasithi; it wiggles its way through the valley, with massive mountains forming a dramatic backdrop.

When the track ends (**1h55min**), a WAYMARKED PATH takes you up over the side of the hill ahead. The way is very rocky here; step carefully to avoid the loose rubble. Winter weather and storms can easily damage the path; you may have to cross some rock slides. Then, after a small area of rock-fall, you will have to negotiate a STRETCH OF SCREE (**2h10min**). Those who suffer from vertigo might find this section unnerving. If you have a head for heights it's a wonderful place to sit, looking out, with sea in the distance to the right and left!

Past the scree you will see a short wall — towards which you are heading. But first you'll have to cross a VERY STEEP DRY RIVER BED — again, some people may find this part of the walk difficult. Then walk along on top of the wall, past a WATER TROUGH and a HUT. Then the way-marked path leads across an open space carpeted in low shrubs. There is a stretch of terrain where the path disappears; look for PAINT WAYMARKS and head diagonally downhill to join the path. You can see it below — running

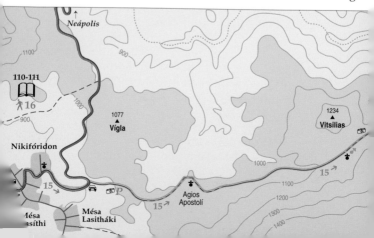

A particularly eye-catching holly oak in the grey-green Lasithi mountains

off to the left over the crest, heading towards Agios Nikolaos. (And, on a clear day, you'll have a lovely, unexpected view of the town itself.) When you approach the far edge of the open area, follow waymarking through a grassy area. Tapes is straight ahead of you now.

The waymarked route peters out as you come down onto a track (**3h35min**). Turn left here. The track rounds three small reservoirs and heads on down to Tapes. Eight minutes from the reservoirs, on a bend to the right, you can take a short-cut trail off to the right (**4h**), which will take you more directly down to Tapes. The stony trail gives way to footpath, winding down past a WINNOWING CIRCLE and crossing a stream bed.

You quickly reach the first buildings of **Tapes** (**4h 05min**), on your right. Walk on past the first group of houses on the left and, just beyond them, fork left downhill. Then turn right. This leads you through the village. A bus stops here occasionally ... just in time to end the Alternative walk.

From here head on downhill, past the CHURCH (now referring to the map on pages 56-57). After a few minutes' walking on a damaged concrete road, you'll come to a *cafeneion* on your right, on the corner of the road where it bends to the left. There is a painted metal spiral stairway on the outside of this cafe (**4h10min**).

To continue on the main walk (and the Short walk) to Kritsa, turn off the road and follow the old concrete trail

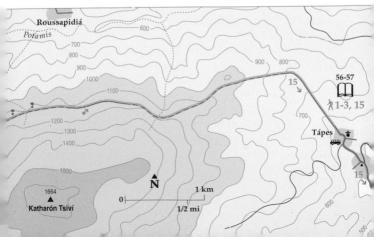

down beside this *cafeneion*. It bends right and, in two minutes, you will be at the edge of the village. By the last house on the right, the way forks: go right on an obvious earthen path heading steeply down into the olive groves in the small valley below. At the bottom of the valley, head right and walk on, going through TWO GATES. After the second gate (within 15 minutes of the olive grove), the easily-seen path leads uphill to the left, becoming an old donkey trail as it rises above the river bed. Ten minutes later, at the top of the rise, you can see the sea at Kalo Horio. Follow the rocky path which runs close to a WALL on your right. Within a minute it bends left, over three low boulders and through a GATEWAY. Continue downhill on the well-defined route, more or less alongside a wall with a fence on top, and heading in the direction of a LARGE CONCRETE STRUCTURE.

Forty minutes from the olive grove (50min from Tapes; **5h**) pass a gateway on your right and come onto a wider track. Ten minutes later continue straight ahead, ignoring a track going back off to the left. Within half a minute go left at a slanting T-junction. Within another minute pass a STONE BUILDING WITH DOUBLE GATES on your right. Continue straight on, ignoring a track going off to the left (almost directly in line with that track, on the hillside in the distance ahead, is the road going up to the site at Lato). Then, just where the track makes a deep curve to the left, go straight ahead — onto a donkey path — keeping the fencing on your right. Follow the donkey trail in a hard bend to the left and then a hard bend back round to the right. Almost immediately the first houses of Kritsa come into view (just over 1h from Tapes; **5h15min**).

When the path comes down onto a track (1h10min from Tapes; **5h20min**), head right towards Kritsa. Five minutes later you will pass the path leading down right to the KRITSA GORGE (followed in Walk 2). Turn left, and continue on track towards the village. When you meet the asphalt road from Lato (1h20min from Tapes; **5h 30min**), turn right over the BRIDGE. The buses turn round and go from a small square up at the far end of the village, so you need to go uphill to the right from the asphalt road. Walk a short way along the road, then turn right up towards the village on a rough track. It narrows and becomes cobbled. When you reach the road that passes through the centre of **Kritsa**, head left downhill again, just past the large church of **Agios Ioannis**, to where the bus turns round (under **6h**).

16 CROSSING THE LASITHI PLATEAU: FROM PSYCHRO TO TZERMIADO

Distance: 6km/3.75mi; 1h35min
Grade: easy, level walking
Equipment: comfortable shoes, sunhat, water
How to get there: 🚌 to Malia (Timetable 1); journey time 30min. Change to 🚌 to the Dikti Cave (Timetable 25); journey time 1h30min. Or by 🚗: park either at the Dikti Cave or at Tzermiado. If you park at the Dikti Cave, take a bus back there from Tzermiado (departs 15.30 Mon, Wed, Fri *only; recheck in advance!*); if you park at Tzermiado, take the Psychro bus to the Dikti Cave to start the walk (departs 09.45 Mon, Wed, Fri *only; recheck in advance!*).
To return: 🚌 from Tzermiado to Malia (Timetable 25), then 🚌 from Malia to Agios Nikolaos (Timetable 1); journey times as above.

You've seen the postcards, now try the walk! It's very straightforward, along the flat. But remember that despite the many postcards showing whirling windmills, they are used for irrigation, and the sails are furled and unfurled only as required. You won't necessarily wander through a myriad of flying sails — although you might be lucky. Even so, you will encounter people at work in the fields, attending to their agricultural round ... and yes, adjusting their windmills.

Leave the bus (or your car) in the large parking area above the village of **Psychro**, where all the buses stop. You'll be able to see your destination — Tzermiado — in the distance. Behind it rises a high mountain with a large rounded top, the setting for Walk 15. You'll keep this in view as you cross the plateau. With your back to the path that goes up to the DIKTI CAVE, **set off** from the parking area in the corner next to the kiosk, heading due northeast on the clear downhill path. It merges into crazy-paving-style steps. To your left is the cemetery and church of Plati. From the steps turn down right to the asphalt road that

The Lasithi Plateau

goes up to the parking area for the cave. There's a taverna on the corner of this road called 'KRONOS' (written in Greek, but easy to decipher). Head left down the road and then straight across two loops of road on a short-cut path.

You'll see a BLUE AND WHITE ROAD SIGN (**5min**), indicating that Agios Nikolaos is to your right and Kato Metohi to the left. Your track lies ahead, across the road. Immediately you're amongst the cultivation of the plateau and will recognise crops of potatoes and courgettes, with scatterings of fruit trees, amongst the chickens and goats. As the way heads to the right (**9min**), no doubt birdsong will accompany you. You cross over a concrete BRIDGE (**11min**), the first of several. There are some sad abandoned windmills along here. To the right you'll see the village of Psychro. Listen out for the busy encouraging hum of working mills, many of which are power-driven. From time to time, you'll hear goats conversing con-

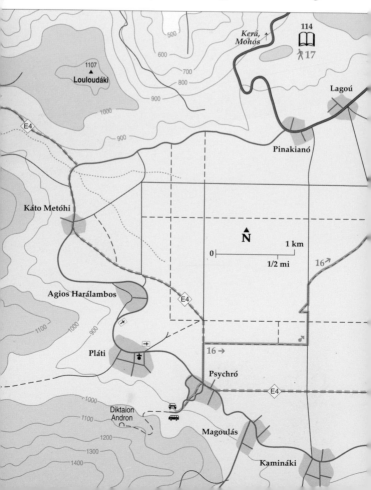

edly, too. Keep straight ahead over an intersection
min), crossing another concrete BRIDGE. Ignore the
ck leading off left three minutes later. Have a look at
 one of the windmills as you pass; it's interesting to see
them working. Eight sails is full power here; six or four
unfurled is quite common.

When another track heads off to the left (**21min**),
ignore it and keep straight ahead. Similarly, keep straight
on a minute later, when a track turns off to the right. You'll
see the village of Magoulas now, up to your right, on the
edge of the plateau. Kaminaki lies just a bit further on,
forming another link in the chain of villages on the fringe
of the plateau.

Go straight over the minor intersection (**25min**) and
another concrete bridge. You may see donkeys tethered,
front and back. This gives them plenty of rope — enough
to go along the ditch at the side of the road, but not enough

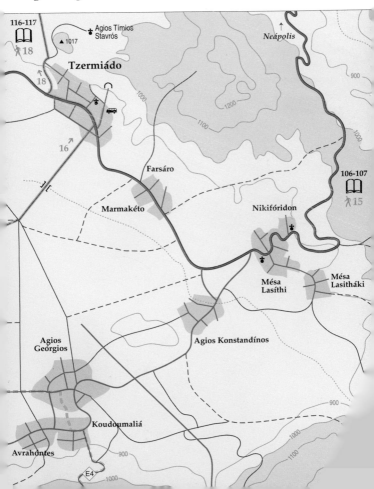

to let them snaffle the crops either side. Very canny. Keep straight on at another intersection (**29min**). Depending on the agricultural calendar, you may identify more crops — onions, runner beans, kale, cabbage, wheat. Whatever the crop, the neat cross-channel irrigation system in the fields creates an attractive picture.

When you come to a CONCRETE WATER STORAGE TANK on your left and a fairly tall apple tree on your right, by another junction (**32min**), turn left. You're now walking towards the northwest side of the plateau, and Tzermiado and the distinctive mountain peaks behind it lie north-northeast. Cross straight over the next intersection (**36min**) and come to a T-junction. Turn left, right, left — all this within a few metres.

Before long (**45min**), you'll be just about in the centre of the plateau. Soon the track bends to the right and then, a minute or so later, to the left. Follow these curves. When the track forks (**55min**), head right. Less than five minutes later, you come to a large intersection: go straight over. Twenty paces further on, ignore the track coming in from the right; keep straight on the main track. In another seven or eight minutes (**1h12min**), go straight over another intersection on a very large BRIDGE. Keep walking straight ahead along a tree-lined avenue. When you come to an intersection with a round stone structure in the middle (**1h25min**), again go straight over. Within five minutes you are on the outskirts of **Tzermiado**. Turn right at the crossroads, then take your first left — on the road past the OTE (telephones). You come to a junction where there is a taverna and *cafeneion* on the right, on the corner (**1h35min**). The bus stops, *briefly*, in the road coming in from the right. Flag it down!

17 KERA TO GONIES

Distance: 9km/5.6mi; 2h
Grade: straightforward track walking, with a descent of 600m/1970ft
Equipment: stout shoes, sunhat, picnic, water
How to get there: 🚌 to Malia (Timetable 1); journey time 30min. Change to Lasithi 🚌 (Timetable 25) and alight at Kera; journey time 1h. Or 🚌 to Gonies and catch the Lasithi 🚌 to Kera to start the walk: departs about 09.30; journey time about 25min.
To return: 🚌 from Gonies to Malia (departs about 14.30, journey time 50min), then 🚌 to Agios Nikolaos (Timetable 1); journey time 30min.

Walking in the foothills of the Selena range, between the Lasithi Plateau and the north coast, is not yet something many people do, attracted by more obvious landscapes. This is a very pleasant, untrammelled countryside jaunt which is enjoyable for flora, fauna — and lovers of peace and quiet.

Alight from the bus at the edge of **Kera**, where it stops by a *cafeneion* on the main road to Lasithi. **Start out** by following the main road up the hill and, on the second large bend, where there is a break in the roadside barrier, take the track that goes off downhill to the right. Very soon there's a tremendous view of the valley into which you will be walking. First of all the walk takes you round the top of it, over to the right. When the track forks (**15min**), keep right downhill.

When you come upon WIRE NETTING, keep bending round to the left; don't take any tracks off to the right. Cross over a concrete surface under which there is a watercourse going down to the right, and ignore a track running back down to the right; keep straight on. At a fork (**30min**), keep right downhill. When you come to a T-junction, turn right (**40min**). After a splash of aggregate surface you will be back on a rough track almost immediately. A few minutes later, keep straight ahead on the

View into the valley, near the start of the walk

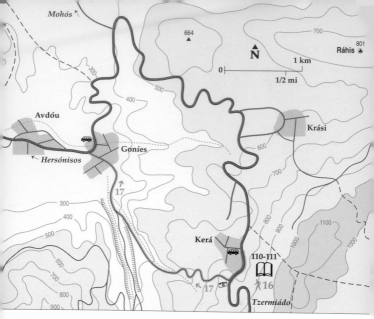

track, ignoring a track going back downhill to the right. Then (**50min**) cross over the watercourse (dry in summer). Here there is an old METAL AND CONCRETE RESERVOIR in the hillside on the left. Just past this reservoir, if you turn round and look back uphill, you will see a line of old mills — at least 18 in all. Next a stunning plug of rock comes into view just up to the left. Within five minutes, at the next fork, go right downhill. You pass a SHRINE and a LITTLE HOUSE off to the right, on a bend (just after **1h**).

As the track bends round to the right and you're almost in the bed of the valley (**1h20min**), look left if you would like to find an old donkey trail which cuts the last main bend off the track. It will be somewhat overgrown in spring so, if you stay on track, continue round the U-bend until you reach the other side of the river valley. The bottom of the valley (**1h40min**) makes perfect grazing ground for flocks but, sadly, it is also perfect for the village rubbish tip. Stay on the flat by the river bed, which should be on your left, all the way to Goníes. As you come to the end of the valley, near tall telegraph poles, keep left at a wide U-fork (**1h50min**), even though you can just see the first houses of Goníes over to the right by the olive trees. The river bed is still on your left. Five minutes past the telegraph poles, at an intersection, turn right and head towards the village houses. Meet the main road, turn right and walk into **Goníes** (**2h**) where there is a supermarket, *cafeneion* and petrol station. The bus stops somewhere near here, wherever it can find a place.

18 TZERMIADO TO VRAHASI

See photograph page 27

Distance: 21km/13mi; 6h10min

Grade: fairly strenuous because of distance; possibility of vertigo. Ascent of 300m/1000ft; descent of 900m/2950ft.

Equipment: stout shoes, long trousers, sunhat, picnic, water

How to get there: 🚌 to Malia (Timetable 1); journey time 30min. Change to 🚌 to Tzermiado (Timetable 25); journey time 1h30min. *To return:* 🚌 from Vrahasi to Agios Nikolaos (Iraklion bus, Timetable 1); journey time about 20min.

Short walk: Tzermiado — Nisimos Plateau — Tzermiado (6km/3.8mi; 2h10min). Easy ascent/descent of 100m/300ft. 🚌 (Timetable 25) or 🚗 to/from Tzermiado. Follow the main walk for 1h10min, then return.

The local people just said 'straight, straight, straight' when we were first trying to find this walk. That's not quite the case, although you certainly have to keep going a fair bit! It's not pioneering, but it is adventurous as walks go — so don't be too exacting about the route —- we've simply traced one of *several* possible ways to do this walk.

From plateau to plain to mountainside, this route provides great vistas for you. Pick a clear day and you will be staggered by the views over north and south from the highest point in the hike — up where you're unlikely to have the company of anything except eagles and goats.

From the bus stop by the OTE (telephone exchange) in **Tzermiado, start out** by retreating a few paces back the way the bus came in. Then turn left (by the SIGN TO THE SANCTUARY CAVE) and left again (opposite the CHURCH), into the main street. Passing the Bank of Crete, continue out of the village and, after the last old terraced house on the right, turn right along a concrete track, where a sign points to the 'TIMIOS STAVROS CHURCH'. (If you reach a large building signed 'KENTPON YΓEIAΣ', you have gone too far.) The way soon becomes a dirt track and takes you past a farmyard. A series of bends takes you slowly uphill, far above the Lasithi Plateau. The views improve round every bend, but watch your step, it's loose and stony underfoot.

The track has ANIMAL PENS either side of it (**20min**); goats, chickens and sheep may be slaking their thirst at the water troughs or resting quietly in pastoral peace under the trees. A gentle breeze may be stirring as you climb; look back at the plateau and pick out the working windmills. Soon you'll notice a band of splendid grey serried rocks, studded with trees and bushes, on your left (**30min**). The track climbs and, up ahead, stone 'portals' frame a tremendous view of the **Nisimos Plateau** and the mountains beyond (Picnic 10). Directly ahead, you'll see the pointed top of Karfi ('Nail') Mountain. The dusty track, kept well cropped by flocks of multi-coloured goats, stretches out across the plain. Stay on the main track and, when you reach the FAR SIDE OF THE PLAIN (**1h10min**; the Short walk turns back here), keep ahead, slightly left.

Go over a low pile of grey rocks and walk across a small flat area. Look up at the mountains ahead; you're going towards the lowest dip on the horizon. Climb over another rock pile and join a goats' path, keeping to the right. The path starts to rise; it's surprising how quickly

you'll climb, even though the going's not hard — just a steady pull.

At a fork (**1h20min**), where there is a rock face ahead of you, go left. In another five minutes you will just be able to see the upper part of Karfi. The path becomes less discernible as the area you're crossing widens out. Head right, towards a grey stony path and carry on up it, curving round towards the right. Soon (**1h30min**) Karfi should be straight ahead of you. You are not heading to its top, but towards its left side. From here there are several paths, but keep beside the ridge to your left. The way flattens out, and you can just about make out the route ahead of you, running across the mountain slope. You will see a distinctive, rounded holly oak tree over to your right, in the middle of a miniature 'valley'. Take a rest under its shade. Then climb up this 'valley' and reach a clearing; Karfi is right in front of you now. But turn back to face the way you've come: you'll have a fantastic view left, to Lasithi in the distance. To your right you can see Malia and Hersonisos on the north coast. The green basin set just back from the coast is Mohos.

Climb up the shoulder, heading towards Karfi. On the ridge to your left you can see a SMALL STONE CONSTRUCTION. Look out for a barely-distinguishable goats' path which traverses the side of the mountain in a northeasterly direction and follow it. The view is breathtaking; you're on top of the world here! Ahead you can see a curved mountain, backed up by a saddle, and then a flat-topped mountain. The path now curves round **Karfi**. Doubtless you'll marvel at the view for a while, identifying all the towns and villages you can spot below. Eagles soar overhead here, keeping watch as you walk on. At this point those who suffer from vertigo may find the path unnerving — there are intermittent stretches where hugging the hillside is difficult. Watch your footing, as the hillside is steep and the path barely trodden.

As you round the mountain, heading northeast (**2h 10min**), look out for a SCREE LINE and cross the top of it, keeping slightly up. Look carefully to find the path going uphill, and soon you will pass a holly oak tree hanging over the route and providing some pleasant shade. You'll find that the path is leading you gradually downhill, as well as across the mountain, which is dotted with holly oaks. (These lovely trees grace many of our mountain walks; see page 107.) Down to your left you can see the track which you will eventually join.

When the path drops down onto the track (**2h45min**), turn right. As you cross over a col (**3h25min**), leave the track and take a small path down to the right (to cut off a bend in the track). In five minutes, go right, back onto the main track. Ignore a track curving off to the left (**3h30min**). You can see the way ahead clearly —- a pleasant change not to have to watch your step all the time. Now you're high up over a valley on the left, and the village of Sisi is in the distance on the coast. Ignore a track to your right (**4h**) leading steeply up yet another mountaintop, and shortly after you will come to a CONCRETE WATER CISTERN on your right.

Having rounded a bend in the track (**4h25min**), you see a path heading off to the right, over rocks, towards a hut and a CONCRETE REPOSITORY that houses forestry department equipment. This is a worthwhile short cut. Pass the concrete construction and turn right back onto the track. A couple more small paths cut loops off the track until you turn right on the main track again (**4h38min**). Soon (**4h45min**) you'll catch your first glimpse of Vrahasi, set above the Iraklion/Agios Nikolaos road. You can even make out the road tunnel just to the right of Vrahasi.

Forking left (just over **5h**), you reach the church of **Agios Georgios** (**5h05min**). Go past the church, keeping it on your right, and stay on the track — which now heads right. You are now walking down the left-hand side of the valley towards Vrahasi. In a few minutes the track divides; take the lower, less-used fork (the church is still on your right). Head downhill on this track for four minutes. Just before it levels out a little and starts to curve to the left, look carefully for a small path, which curls back down to the right. Zigzag downhill here for two minutes — almost to the floor of the valley — sometimes on path, sometimes on overgrown track. You will then drop down to a more obvious track. Follow it to the left, once again going down into the valley and away from the church. Five minutes later, when the track divides, go left.

After five minutes you will notice that the valley has dropped away below you. Don't worry if you appear to be heading uphill a little. After five more minutes the track curves round into the bottom of the valley and crosses the watercourse; continue by curving around to the left, on the track. A number of tracks merge into the one you are on; ignore them. When you come to a fork, head uphill to the right. Half an hour from Agios Georgios (**5h35min**), meet a crossing track and go straight over it, onto a small path heading downhill. Now you can see and hear the road. Bear left, cross the watercourse when you meet it, and climb uphill. Go left at a T-junction. Soon you join a wider track. Arriving at the main road in **Vrahasi** (50min from Agios Georgios; **6h**), turn right. Ten minutes along you'll see the BUS SHELTER and stop (**6h10min**).

Distance: 14km/8.7mi; 4h25min

Grade: fairly strenuous, with a long steep ascent of 680m/2230ft and descent of 560m/1840ft; however, the terrain is not difficult. A wire fence to scramble over.

Equipment: stout shoes, sunhat, water, picnic

How to get there and return: 🚗 to 'Embaros: park in the main square. Return on 🚌 from Ano Viannos to 'Embaros (Iraklion bus; Timetable 24): departs Ano Viannos at about 17.30 *Mon-Fri only (recheck!)*; journey time about 20min. While the walk is also *possible* by bus via Iraklion (Timetable 24), this would make for a *very* long day.

Short walk: to Miliaradon's gorge and return (3.5km/2mi; 1h35min). Fairly strenuous climb of 200m/725ft; equipment as above; 🚗 to/from Miliaradon: park by the church. Follow the main walk from the 30min-point to the 1h20min-point (or a little further) and return the same way.

Although it's not one of our longest walks, this expe-dition gives you a good (and fairly full) day's outing, because of the distances involved. We'd suggest that you combine the walk with Car tour 8, driving to 'Embaros via Hersonisos and Kasteli and returning via Ierapetra. This big loop guarantees that you take in a great slice of landscape in one day. Pick a clear day for the walk, and you'll be able to see forever! It's a long pull up the mountain from Miliaradon, but when you're finally on the heights you'll feel on top of the world, with great spreads of sky and land stretching out for miles around you.

Start out in open main square at **'Embaros**. With a *cafeneion* (currently with white pillars) on your right and the POST OFFICE and some huge telephone poles behind you to the left, turn left: follow the road SIGNPOSTED FOR MILIARADON. It curves round to the right. When the road forks by a SIGN TO XENIAKOS (**10min**), go right and, five minutes later, turn right over a BRIDGE. Fifteen minutes later you will pass the sign at the beginning of **Miliaradon**, and the road curves through the village to the CHURCH (**30min**). Turn left opposite the church (ignoring a branch-off to the right), and walk up between the village houses. The path is steep and rough. Three minutes above the last house, ignore a fork to the right and go straight ahead uphill (there is a red WAYMARK indicating the route here).

After a few minutes, continue by following a stone wall to your right. You are still in the olive tree belt. Very soon you will cross a track; keep straight ahead, following the footpath (red arrow WAYMARK). The direction is due south, towards the left-hand side of the peak facing you. The path you are on widens out, looking more like a track. Stay on it, as indicated by the red WAYMARKS, and ignore a path leading to the right.

About 15 minutes beyond Miliaradon, after a hairpin bend in the track, follow a small short-cut path to the left. Soon rejoining the track, follow it to the left. A minute later, at a fork, go right, taking a WAYMARKED PATH through tall grass. After a minute, at a fork, turn left, as the way-marking indicates. You pass a small vineyard on the left and almond and olive trees on the right. Soon, at a STONE WALL, turn left. After a couple of minutes, at a fork, go uphill to the right. (This point is marked by a particularly large and IMPRESSIVE ROCK.)

You come upon a flattish area at the edge of the hillside (**1h**), with a RUINED STONE DWELLING to your far right. Just beyond the dwelling there is a good view of the bottom

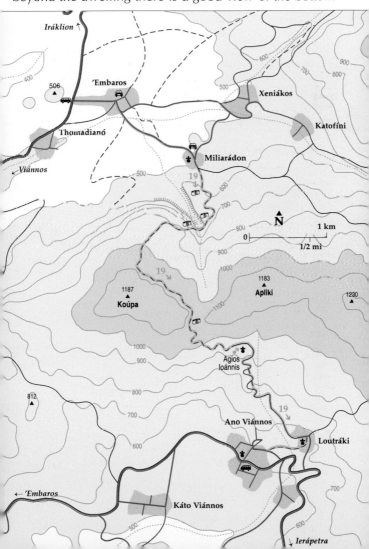

In 1h35min, from a large rock buttress, you enjoy a fine view back down over Miliaradon.

of the gorge. This is a nice place to take a break or enjoy a picnic … in half an hour's time you'll be looking down on this spot from the top of the gorge!

At this point, the track makes a hairpin turn. Just after this turn, leave the track and take the narrow footpath off to your right; there is a stone wall to the left of this path. You are now leaving the olive trees behind you. After a few minutes, the stone wall ends. Keep ahead, veering slightly towards the right-hand side of the hill. Soon, on meeting a small fork, go left; then go left again at a second small fork.

You are now heading towards the top and left-hand side of the hill. You will come to a gate and a three-way junction surrounded by wire fences (**1h15min**). Go through the gate and then straight ahead uphill. The WAYMARKING is still with you. To your right you can see the cliff and, further to the right, below you, a small valley. Follow the path, with the wire fence is still on your left. As the path leads you around the edge of the ravine, you can see it continuing up to the precipice ahead.

Soon (**1h20min**), from a large rock buttress on your left, you will have a good view down the valley and out over flat land (see photograph above). As the path curves around the valley, you will pass a large holly oak tree to your right, where you can rest and enjoy the view. End the Short walk here — or 10 minutes later, when the path flattens out, signalling the end of this climb. As the path continues uphill, those who suffer from vertigo should take care as they near the end of this gorge. Although the path doesn't run along the edge (it's at least 10m/yds away), it's very high.

Walking onwards and upwards, you reach the top of the cliff — at a point where the valley turns into a narrow steep ravine. The torrents of water must be furious here in winter. Looking to your right, beyond the precipice, you can see Miliaradon in the distance. Cross the valley near here, where the precipice becomes flatter. You will pass through a STOCK CONTROL GATE. Seven minutes later, while walking essentially parallel to the edge of the cliff, you reach a group of prominent holly-oak trees. Five minutes later you pass a small stream bed. The path veers to the left, away from the edge of the cliff, and follows the right-hand side of this STREAM BED. Walking through some bushes, strikingly distorted by the frequent strong winds, you approach a SHEPHERD'S HUT (**1h50min**). Your arrival may be heralded by a pack of barking dogs, running loose. The barking is ferocious, but talk to them and walk on, and they'll soon leave you alone (see page 49).

As you pass to the left of the hut, you can take a look at the Koupa peak ahead. At this point, when you meet a track, follow it to the left. A couple of minutes later, fork right on another track. After a few paces you will pass some stone SHEPHERDS' HUTS on either side of the track. Follow the track as it turns to the left here. About 13 minutes later, after passing another SHEPHERD'S HUT on the right, the track ends by yet another STONE HUT, this time deserted (**2h05min**). Follow the path heading in the same direction. Four minutes later, you pass a holly-oak tree and cross a dry STREAM BED. The path now becomes less distinct, but your direction is clear — you are heading towards a group of pointed white-looking rocks a few hundred metres/yards away. You can see a wire fence to the left of those rocks, which in fact extends for kilometres either way. This is a tricky point in the walk, as there is no gate, and you will have to climb over the fence at its weakest point. Fifteen minutes later, when you reach the rocks, find a low/weak point in the fence and go over it. (Alternatively, you can follow the fence along to the right and cross it close to the col described in the next paragraph.)

Take stock of your surroundings now. Behind you is the valley where the Short walk ended; in front of you, in the distance and to the left of the fence you just crossed, is another, larger group of whitish boulders. These are at the col between the Koupa and Apliki peaks. At this point you want to make for the right-hand side of these boulders. A path is visible a bit further ahead, leading to them. Ten minutes later, you reach those rocks at the COL between **Koupa** and **Apliki** (**2h30min**). The view is panoramic, with vistas both north and south. The village of Ano Viannos is visible to the left in a south-southeasterly direction.

Look to the left, facing the distant south coast that has just come into sight, and you'll see your continuing path, easily discernible. Look left, at the boulders here, and you will spot the WAYMARK. Hedgehog-like mounds of Jerusalem sage and thorny burnet are all around you in this wonderfully scenic setting. There's a tremendous view over the plain, which is thickly cloaked in trees.

Walk left across the top of the ridge; the WAYMARKING is still with you. The track starting the descent down this side of the mountain leads you to a NETTING FENCE. Walk alongside it until you see a GATE. Go through the fence here, and take the downhill path. Twelve paces from the fence you'll see a waymark. For a while you will lose sight of the plains, and then Ano Viannos comes into sight, far below to your right. You will pass a distinctive outcrop of greenish rock on the path (**2h50min**). Once you're past these green rocks, you must look carefully for the waymarking leading you down (rather than across) the hillside. Follow the zigzags. At this point, you can see a track below you, which you join in about five minutes. Follow this track downhill: six minutes along, another track comes in from the right, and you find yourself in front of an IRON GATE. Go through the gate and continue straight on. A few minutes later, you pass a THRESHING CIRCLE on the right.

Before too long you will have dropped down amongst olive and fruit trees and then you will see the roof of a little chapel, **Agios Ioannis** (**3h25min**). There is a SPRING here, where you can rest under the shade of the trees. Follow the track past the church, then leave it at a small building just beyond the church, heading left into an unkempt olive grove. Go left again almost immediately, until you meet a small STONE WALL. Follow the wall, keeping it to your right, heading downhill among the trees until, a couple of minutes later, you meet the track again. Join it and turn left. Follow it for three bends, then take the path off left which, within a few paces, has a wall on its right.

It's likely that you will have come all this way without

On the descent from the col

having set eyes on another living soul — except perhaps a shepherd or someone tending crops outside Ano Viannos. The peace and stillness is sublime. The path now leads down beside a river valley on the left, thick with chestnut and cypress trees thriving on their moisture-holding base. The red daubs have deserted you by this time. Cross the WATERCOURSE (**3h 35min**) and round a bend, to find yourself on the other side of the river — it's on your right.

Anos Viannos nestles ahead between the hills, framed by the luxuriant foliage of the valley. You reach a CHURCH on your right (**3h45min**); this is the outskirts of **Loutraki**. Take the small, loose-stone path on your right just past the church (having first walked a few steps on asphalt to pass the church). After 10 minutes, when this path divides, go left and curve downhill. Chicken huts and animal shelters signal the first buildings of **Ano Viannos** (**4h**). Here you descend onto a cobbled path. Turn left, heading down past more old buildings; then turn right. Keep descending and you'll come into the main square. The bus stops almost opposite the CHURCH (**4h10min**).

The bus will drop you at a junction on the main road; follow signposting back into the square at **'Embaros** (**4h25min**), to collect your car.

Distance: 13km/8mi; 4h. But note that you could also start the walk at Mithi, saving 2km (30min).

Grade: strenuous, with some steep climbing up and around three gorges; tight schedule. Overall ascent 550m/1800ft.

Equipment: stout shoes or boots, sunhat, picnic, water

How to get there: 🚌 to Ierapetra (Timetable 5); journey time under 1h. Then taxi from Ierapetra to Mournies (or Mithi, if you are starting there). Plan to start the walk by 10.45 at the latest, in order to reach Males in time for the only afternoon bus.

To return: 🚌 from Males to Agios Nikolaos (not in the timetables): departs 15.00 *Mon-Fri only (recheck!);* journey time 40min.

Three gorges in one walk! Need we say that there are some awesome and breathtaking landscapes on the route from Mournies to Males? It's very obvious that the earth has risen up and writhed about in aeons past, before settling into the dramatic forms you'll see on this walk. The route takes you not only through all this splendid upheaval, but onto the pine-covered hillsides linking four villages strung out across this most attractive pocket of Eastern Crete. You really can't afford to dally on this hike, unfortunately: there's a tight bus connection at the end. Your pace needs to be steady. You must press on. So do not attempt it if you feel at all fainthearted.

There are no convenient buses to Mournies, only to Mirtos, 5km away, which has no taxis, so the best option for this walk is to take a taxi from Ierapetra. **Start out** in the VILLAGE SQUARE at **Mournies**. From the square keep right on the road to Mithi, ignoring a route up to the left. Quickly leaving Mournies (**5min**), the descending road heads for the hills. Soon (**10min**), when you can see a mountain panorama in front of you, ignore the route bending up to the left. Straight ahead is your destination, Males. Ten minutes later you pass a lovely setting when you're walking through olive trees, with views towards massive mountain folds ahead (**20min**). You can also see the villages of Mithi, in the foreground, and Males beyond, to the left — looking far closer than it is!

When you come into **Mithi** (**30min**), the CHURCH is on your right. Just before coming upon a barrage of signposts, turn left uphill, out of the village — a steep climb. At the top, take the central route. Very soon the track divides: take the right-hand track — the one which goes between an olive tree on your left and a carob tree on your right. This track leads you past a small house. When the track divides again (**40min**), take the left-hand, higher track. There's a lovely picnic setting here, under a big tree, with views over the distinctive mountain folds. Later there's another fantastic view down into the deep Sarakini Gorge running back to the Libyan Sea (**55min**). Just the start of things to come!

From this point, you will keep on this main track for about another 10 minutes, so ignore any smaller tracks leading off it. Having passed a wire fence, you can see a lone, island-like rock rising opposite a deep, impressive gorge (**1h**). The track now appears to be leading you back

Fresh-scented pines frame the view over the first gorge en route.

towards the village; don't worry, it is just taking you past the hill, so keep on following it. When the track ends (**1h05min**), start climbing to the right, up a steep narrow path, which starts beside a small STONE WALL and a WIRE FENCE. (A stone CAIRN *may* still be there to show you the way.) Soon, at a clearing, you come to a break in the wire fence: do not follow the path ahead, but head left along the fence until you come to a STOCK CONTROL GATE. Go through it and then keep straight ahead. The path now

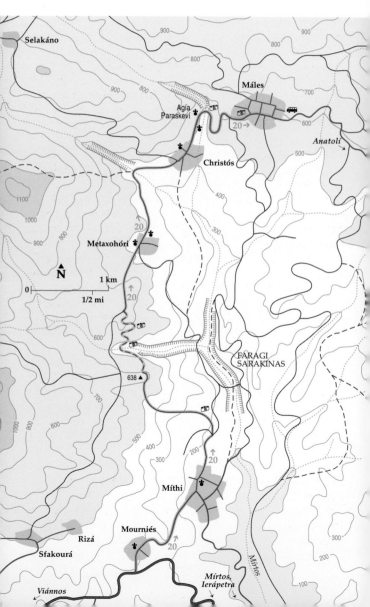

leads you through bright green, fresh-scented pines — via the enormous gorge shown on page 127. Huge rocks rear up from inside it; imagine the geological upheaval that created all this splendour.

When you come to a river bed, where the head of the gorge is straight in front of you (**1h35min**), cross the river bed and start up the other side on a steep rocky path, from where the views are especially fine. But watch your footing; you may have to step over a small landslide here. Ten minutes later there are fantastic views of the surrounding country from the far side of a huge boulder at the right of the path. Reaching the top of this climb (**1h45min**), the path levels out. Look to the right again, for more splendid views over the gorge and the hills beyond it, down to the sea. Go straight towards the hill rising in the distance in front of you, bearing in mind that your general direction is Males. The path takes you round the right-hand side of the hill, narrowing and overgrown where vegetation has encroached. You really are off the beaten track! Look out for a stock-control gate below the hill and go through it, veering to the right of the hill. In places the path is still cobbled, but it's mostly overgrown. At the top of the rise, beyond a small stone wall, walk to the left of a WINNOWING CIRCLE, where you will meet a track. Turn right and follow this track, soon ignoring a track that leads off abruptly to the right. Before long you will see a couple of buildings to your right. Your track will merge with a track going past an old stone dwelling below to the right, and shortly you will see the first hamlet en route, Metaxohori, followed by Christos and then Males to the far right. Join another track (**2h25min**) and keep straight on into the ramshackle hamlet of **Metaxohori**. There's not much sign of life here.

Leave the village on the track curving down to the right; there's an old CHURCH up to the left and a newer one further down, to the right. Follow the main route. As you near the end of the next gorge (**2h45min**), the track has a very steep drop down to one side. There are huge boulders strewn about; what havoc they must have caused when they rolled down the hill.

Eventually you reach a first sign announcing **Christos** (**3h10min**). This is a very fertile area, with water flowing in off the banks across your path. The contrast between Christos and Metaxohori is marked: although it's also an old and slightly dilapidated village (even the church tower leans over), Christos is very definitely thriving.

When you come to another sign for this straggling village, take the left-hand, higher track.

If you feel you're behind schedule, at the end of the next wide bend, take the narrow short-cut path up to the right. After a minute, step across the water channel and climb sharply up to the left, on a narrow path along the edge of the channel, then go right, past a water barrel. Zigzag up to meet the road.

Whichever way you take, turn away from the village and the distant sea and walk along the road. Round the corner you'll see a pretty church below in the gorge, and you'll be accompanied by the sound of gurgling water. Soon you can make a pleasant, albeit brief, 'pit stop' at a very quaint taverna. It sits on a raised square, where the very tiny church of **Agia Paraskevi** nestles beside a huge tree, and a gushing spring is used to cool bottles. Not far past here, the road (still with water pouring down the banks onto it) curves round the end of yet another gorge.

As you curve round towards Males (**3h50min**), drink in the views over to the right: you've walked over all those hills from the far-distant sea. A little further on, pause again to look down over the remains of a village set below to the right.

You might be tempted by a sign (the back of which you'll see first, on your left) pointing the way back to Mithi — 12km down to the right. While the distance is really more like only 8km, we suggest you finish the walk by continuing up the road to **Males** (**4h**). On entering the village, curve left up the main street, past a *cafeneion* on the right. Walk to the end of the village; there are just a couple of houses on the left and an open area where the bus turns round. Here you pick up the *only* return bus of the day. It could be early, and the bus drivers are not inclined to wait — they don't even turn the engine off. The bus ride back to Agios Nikolaos is wonderfully scenic. Just before the village of Anatoli, another bus waits for the one you're on. It goes on to Ierapetra — in case you're staying in the south and this suits you better.

21 SAMARIA GORGE FROM AGIOS NIKOLAOS

See photograph page 53

Distance (of walk): 18km/11.2mi; 4-6h

Open: April/May to October (depending on winter rainfall)

Grade: strenuous, particularly if you're not used to walking; the descent is over 1200m/4000ft.

Equipment: walking boots or stout shoes, sunhat, water bottle (in which to collect spring water), picnic, swimming things

How to get there and return: organised tour (see text below); the price of the ticket includes the boat trip along the coast for your return bus.

It's hard to resist the Samaria challenge and, although it's a long and tiring day, it will also be an unforgettable and exhilarating achievement for you! The scenery is spectacular. Don't go down helter-skelter, trying to beat any records; take the walk at a leisurely pace and enjoy the flowers, the birds and the stunning landscape of the Levka Ori ('White Mountains'), as you wander through their depths.

Important note: **Do not** try to find a different route to the sea and do not leave the designated path through the gorge. **This is imperative!**

There are frequent excursions to the Samaria Gorge organised by tour operators in Agios Nikolaos and other tourist centres on Crete. (You could also take a hired car to Hania, but that would involve an overnight stay.) What

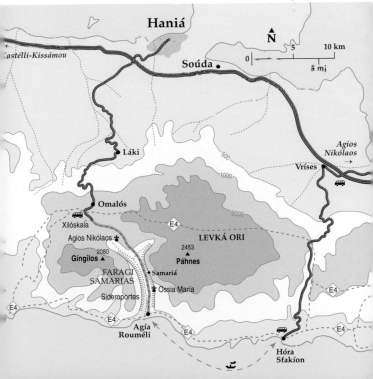

a wonderful overview of Cretan landscapes you'll enjoy on this excursion — with two bus journeys and a boat ride to boot! Your day starts at about 05.00, when you meet your tour bus — at your own hotel or one near your accommodation. (Your day will end at about 23.00.) From the outskirts of Hania, the bus turns south to the Omalos (the 'Plain'), where it invariably makes a breakfast stop — thick, creamy yoghurt and Cretan honey. Then there's a further short ride to the top of the gorge, 1220m/4000ft above sea level.

You **start the walk** on the wooden staircase *(xiloskala)*, an ingenious construction built from tree trunks. On your right, the huge wall of grey rock is **Gingilos** Mountain; it rears up menacingly overhead. The staircase becomes a path and drops down some 1000m/3250ft to the bottom of the upper gorge — and you're still only two kilometres into the walk! After you pass the small chapel of **Agios Nikolaos**, set amongst pines and cypresses to the right, the route becomes less steep.

At about the halfway mark, you come into the old hamlet of **Samaria**. One of the buildings (into which you can go and sign the visitors' book) has been restored for the wardens who succeeded the original inhabitants when the gorge was designated a national park. This is a popular resting point. From here you'll continue past the church of **Ossia Maria** (the 'Bones of Mary') and then through the famous 'Iron Gates' (**Sideroportes**), where the gorge is at its narrowest and the rock walls soar straight up 325m/1000ft either side of you. Be prepared to take your shoes off here and paddle across the Tarraios River, which is so full in winter that the gorge is closed.

The walk ends where the river meets the sea, at **Agia Roumeli**. You can swim from the beach here before taking your boat to Hora Sfakion, an hour away. Then the coach will meet you again for the return journey.

After the other walks we've traced out in this book you'll doubtless find Samaria a busy thoroughfare — at times even overcrowded. You certainly won't lose your way either, with all the other people following the same well-worn route. At least you won't have to follow a step by-step set of instructions...

No doubt on the boat trip to Hora Sfakion you will decide to return and explore this area with the help of *Landscapes of Western Crete*. And who knows — you may even introduce some fellow walkers to the pleasures of rambling off the beaten track in *Eastern* Crete.

BUS TIMETABLES

(See Index to quickly locate timetable number for each destination; see plans on pages 8-9 for location of bus stations).

BUSES FROM AGIOS NIKOLAOS

1 Agios Nikolaos — Malia — Hersonisos — Iraklion; daily; journey 1h30min
Departures from Agios Nikolaos: 06.30, 07.30, 08.00, 09.00*, 09.30, 10.30, 11.00, 11.30, 12.00, 12.30*, 13.00, 13.30, 14.00, 14.30, 15.00, 15.30, 16.00, 16.30, 17.00, 18.00, 19.15, 20.15, 21.00, 22.15
Departures from Iraklion: 06.30*, 07.00, 07.30, 08.00, 08.30, 09.00, 09.30, 10.00, 10.30, 11.00, 11.30, 12.30, 13.00, 13.30, 14.30, 15.00, 15.30, 16.30, 17.30, 18.30, 19.30, 20.00, 21.00, 22.00

2 Agios Nikolaos — Elounda — Shisma; journey 15min
Mondays to Fridays
Departures from Agios Nikolaos: 06.15, 07.15, 08.45, 09.30, 10.00, 10.30, 11.00, 11.30, 12.00, 13.00, 14.00, 14.30, 15.00, 16.00, 17.00, 18.00, 19.00, 20.00, 21.00
Departures from Shisma: 07.30, 09.20, 09.50, 10.20, 10.50, 11.35, 11.50, 12.20, 13.35, 14.20, 15.35, 16.20, 17.35, 18.20, 19.35, 20.20, 21.20
Saturdays, Sundays and holidays
Departures from Agios Nikolaos: 07.15, 08.45, 10.00, 11.00, 12.00, 13.00, 14.00, 15.00, 16.00, 17.00, 18.00, 19.00, 20.00, 21.00
Departures from Shisma: 07.30, 09.20, 10.20, 11.35, 12.20, 13.35, 14.20, 15.35, 16.20, 17.35, 18.20, 19.35, 20.20, 21.20

3 Agios Nikolaos to Kritsa; journey 15min
Mondays to Fridays
Departures from Agios Nikolaos: 06.00, 07.00, 08.00, 10.15, 11.15, 12.15, 13.00, 14.00, 14.30, 16.30, 19.00
Departures from Kritsa: 06.30, 07.30, 08.15, 10.30, 11.30, 12.30, 13.30, 14.15, 15.00, 17.00, 19.30
Saturdays, Sundays and holidays
Departures from Agios Nikolaos: 06.00, 10.15, 11.15, 12.15, 14.00, 16.30, 19.00
Departures from Kritsa: 06.30, 10.30, 11.30, 12.30, 14.15, 17.00, 19.15

4 Agios Nikolaos — Neapolis — Lasithi Plateau (Diktaion or 'Dikti' Cave); Mon, Wed, Fri only; journey 1h30min
Departs Agios Nikolaos: 14.00
Departs Dikti Cave: 07.00

5 Agios Nikolaos — Istron — Gournia — Ierapetra; daily; journey 1h
Departures from Agios Nikolaos: 06.30, 09.00, 10.00**, 11.00, 13.00, 15.00, 17.00, 19.00, 21.00
Departures from Ierapetra: 06.30, 08.30, 10.30, 12.30, 14.30, 15.30, 16.00, 17.00, 18.15, 20.00
*not Sundays; **not Saturdays or Sundays

6 Agios Nikolaos — Istron — Gournia — Sitia; daily; journey 1h30min
Departures from Agios Nikolaos: 06.15, 08.30, 10.00, 12.00, 14.00, 18.00
Departures from Sitia: 06.15**, 09.15, 12.30, 14.45, 17.30, 20.00

7 Agios Nikolaos — Elounda — Plaka; daily; journey 40min
Departures from Agios Nikolaos: 08.45, 11.00, 13.00, 14.30**, 15.00, 17.00, 19.00
Departures from Plaka: 09.15, 11.30, 13.30, 15.30, 17.30, 19.30

BUSES FROM SITIA

8 Sitia to Iraklion via Agios Nikolaos; daily; journey 3h15min
Departures from Sitia: 06.15, 09.15, 12.30, 14.45, 17.30
Departures from Iraklion: 07.00, 08.30, 10.30, 12.30, 16.30

9 Sitia — Palekastro — Vai; daily; journey 1h
Departures from Sitia: 09.30, 11.00, 12.00, 13.00, 14.30, 16.00
Departures from Vai: 10.15, 13.00, 13.30, 16.00, 18.00

10 Sitia — Makrigialos — Ierapetra; daily; journey 1h30min
Departures from Sitia: 09.00, 12.15, 14.15, 18.00, 20.00
Departures from Ierapetra: 08.00**, 09.30, 12.15, 14.15, 20.00

11 Sitia — Palekastro — Kato Zakros; daily; journey 1h
Departures from Sitia: 06.00 (only to Zakros), 11.00, 14.30**
Departures from Kato Zakros: 13.00**, 16.00

BUSES FROM IRAKLION

12 Iraklion — Hersonisos — Malia; daily; journey 1h; from Station A (near the harbour)
Departures from Iraklion: from 06.30 to 22.00 half-hourly (every 15min from 08.30 to 11.00 and from 14.00 to 17.30, except Sundays)
Departures from Malia: from 07.00 to 23.00 half-hourly (every 15min from 09.30 to 12.30 and from 15.00 to 18.00, except Sundays)

13 Iraklion to Agios Nikolaos; daily; journey 1h30min; from Station A (near the harbour)
See Timetable 1

14 Iraklion — Agios Nikolaos — Gournia — Ierapetra; daily; journey 2h30min; from Station A (near the harbour)
Departures from Iraklion: 07.30, 08.30**, 09.30, 11.30, 13.30, 15.30, 17.30, 19.30

Departures from Ierapetra: 06.30, 08.30, 10.30, 12.30, 14.30, 15.30, 16.00**, 17.00, 18.15, 20.00

15 Iraklion — Agios Nikolaos — Gournia — Sitia; daily; journey 3h15min; from Station A (near the harbour)
See Timetable 8

16 Iraklion — Lasithi Plateau (Diktaion or 'Dikti' Cave); daily; journey 2h; from Station A (near the harbour)
Departures from Iraklion: 08.30, 15.00*
Departures from Diktaion Cave: 07.00**, 14.00, 16.45*

17 Iraklion to Arhanes; daily; journey 30min; from Station A (near the harbour)
Departures from Iraklion: 06.30**, 07.00, 07.30**, 08.00*, 08.30***, 09.00*, 10.00, 11.00**, 12.00, 13.00*, 14.00*, 15.00, 16.00**, 17.00, 19.00*, 20.30**
Departures from Arhanes: 06.30*, 07.00**, 17.30, 08.00**, 08.30*, 09.00, 10.00*, 11.00, 12.00**, 13.00, 14.00*, 15.00**, 16.00, 17.00**, 18.00, 20.00*

18 Iraklion to Agia Pelagia; daily; journey 30min; from Station A (near the harbour)
Departures from Iraklion: 08.15, 08.45, 09.45, 11.15, 14.30, 17.00, 19.00
Departures from Agia Pelagia: 09.00, 09.30, 10.30, 12.00, 15.15, 17.45, 19.45

19 Iraklion to Festos; journey 1h30min; from Station B (outside the Hania Gate)
Mondays to Fridays
Departures from Iraklion: 07.30, 09.00, 10.15, 10.30, 11.30, 12.30, 14.00, 15.30, 16.30, 18.00
Departures from Festos: 09.45, 10.30, 11.45, 12.30, 13.30, 13.45, 14.45, 15.30, 16.45, 17.30, 19.15, 20.15

Saturdays, Sundays and holidays
Departures from Iraklion: 07.30, 09.00, 09.30, 10.30, 11.30, 12.30, 14.00, 15.30, 16.30, 18.00
Departures from Festos: 09.45, 10.30, 11.45, 12.30, 13.30, 13.45, 14.45, 15.30, 16.45, 17.30, 19.15, 20.15

20 Iraklion to Agia Galini; daily; journey 2h15min; from Station B (outside the Hania Gate)
Departures from Iraklion: 06.30**, 07.30, 09.00, 10.30, 12.30, 14.00, 16.30, 19.30 (only to Tybaki)
Departures from Agia Galini (Mon-Fri): 08.00, 09.30, 11.30, 13.15, 15.00, 16.15, 18.45
Departures from Agia Galini (Sat, Sun, holidays): 08.00, 10.00, 12.00, 13.15*, 15.00, 16.15, 18.45

21 Iraklion to Matala; journey 2h; from Station B (outside the Hania Gate)
Mondays to Fridays
Departures from Iraklion: 07.30, 09.00, 10.15, 11.30, 12.30, 13.00, 15.30, 18.00
Departures from Matala: 07.00, 09.30,11.30, 13.15, 14.30, 17.15, 20.00
Saturdays, Sundays and holidays
Departures from Iraklion: 07.30, 09.30, 10.15*, 11.30, 12.30, 13.00*, 15.30, 18.00
Departures from Matala: 07.00*, 09.30,11.30*, 13.15, 14.30, 17.15, 20.00

BUSES FROM IERAPETRA
(See also Timetables 5, 14)

22 Ierapetra to Makrigialos; journey 30min
Mondays to Fridays
Departures from Ierapetra: 06.15, 08.00, 09.30, 10.15, 12.15, 13.15, 14.15, 18.00, 20.00
Departures from Makrigialos: 07.00, 09.45, 11.00, 13.00, 14.00, 15.00, 18.45, 20.45
Saturdays, Sundays and holidays
Departures from Ierapetra: 06.30, 09.30, 12.15, 14.15, 18.00, 20.00
Departures from Makrigialos: 09.15, 09.45, 13.00, 15.00, 18.45, 20.45

23 Ierapetra to Mirtos; journey 30min
Mondays to Fridays
Departures from Ierapetra: 06.00, 10.30, 12.30, 14.15, 16.30, 20.00
Departures from Mirtos: 07.00, 10.50, 12.50, 14.50, 16.50, 20.20
Saturdays, Sundays and holidays
Departures from Ierapetra: 08.00*, 10.30, 12.30
Departures from Mirtos: 08.20*, 10.50, 12.50

24 Ierapetra — Viannos — Iraklion; journey 2h30min
Mondays and Fridays only
Departures from Ierapetra: 06.00, 16.30
Departures from Iraklion: 09.30, 15.00

BUS FROM MALIA
(See also Timetables 1, 12)

25 Malia — Hersonisos — Lasithi Plateau (Diktaion or 'Dikti' Cave); daily; journey 1h30min
Departures from Malia: 08.30
Departures from Dikti Cave: 14.00, 16.45*

*not Sundays; **not Saturdays or Sundays; ***only Saturdays and Sundays

☀ Index

Geographical names are the only entries in this index. For other entries, see Contents, page 3. A page number in *italic type* indicates a map; a page number in **bold type** indicates a photograph. Both of these may be in addition to a text reference on the same page. 'TT' means Bus Timetable number; note that the numbers following TT are *timetable numbers, not page numbers*. The Bus Timetables are on pages 133-134. Pronunciation: the syllable to be stressed is indicated by ´ (for example: Almirós/Almi**rós**).